# A Moral Emergency: Breaking the Cycle of Child Sexual Abuse

Jade Christine Angelica

**Sheed & Ward**

Sheed & Ward™ is a service of The National Catholic Reporter Publishing Company.

---

**Library of Congress Cataloguing in Publication Data**

Angelica, Jade C. (Jade Christine), 1952-
    A moral emergency : breaking the cycle of child sexual abuse / Jade C. Angelica.
       p. cm.
    Includes bibliographical references.
    ISBN 1-55612-617-4
    1. Sexually abused children--Pastoral counseling of. 2. Adult child sexual abuse victims--Pastoral counseling of. 3. Child molesting--Religious aspects--Christianity. 4. Child molesting--Prevention. I. Title.
BV4464.3.A535 1993
261.8'32--dc20
                                       93-939
                                        CIP

---

Published by:  Sheed & Ward
                 115 E. Armour Blvd.
                 P.O. Box 419492
                 Kansas City, MO 64141-6492

To order, call: (800) 333-7373

# Contents

*To:*

*Steve, Catherine, Susan, Annamarie, Elizabeth, Joe,*
*Hannah, Chloe, Faith, Barbara, Shane, Chris, Gayle,*
*Richard, Charlotte, Ann, Karen, Kathy, Beth, Karen,*
*Lucy, Stephen, Pat, Jane, Daniel, Nancy, Lee, Terri,*
*Eve, Linda, Jayne,*
*and*
*all of our Sisters and Brothers in survival,*


*and to:*

*my cousin, Pat,*
*with thanks for being a "Glimmer of Hope"*

# *Acknowledgments*

There are many people to acknowledge and to thank . . . many survivors who shared their lives with me, many professionals, from vastly different disciplines, who shared their knowledge with me, many colleagues and friends who enlightened and encouraged me, many teachers who learned along with me about the issue of child sexual abuse. I thank you all.

I would like to especially acknowledge a few of the many. Without the presence of any one of them in my life, this book would not have been completed.

The Reverend Libbie Stoddard
Unitarian Universalist Fellowship
Lafayette, Indiana

Thank you Libbie, for your commitment to the issue of child sexual abuse; for the work you're doing with survivors; for the sermons you've delivered; for the workshops and trainings you've developed; and for the ones you've helped me to develop. Thank you for your consistent thoughtfulness and your attention to people as well as to details. Thank you for listening. Thank you for being my friend and mentor.

Mark U. Edwards, Jr.
Professor of the History of Christianity
Harvard Divinity School
Cambridge, Massachusetts

Thank you Mark, first for your skepticism which challenged me to be thorough in my historical research, and then for your praise for a job well done. Thank you also for encouraging me to expand my historical research into what became the first draft of the present manuscript. Thank you for guiding me throughout that process.

The Reverend Dudley C. Rose,
Associate Director of Ministerial Studies
Harvard Divinity School
Cambridge, Massachusetts

Thank you Dudley, for everything . . . for your insights, your support, your guidance, your holy presence . . . as I grappled with psychological and theological issues surrounding the issue of child sexual abuse. Our work together gave my perspective a broader and deeper understanding of human relationships.

The Reverend Christina Culver
Maynard, Massachusetts

Thank you Chris, most importantly, for your friendship. The time and energy you spent working with me as I created the first draft of this manuscript was both precious and fruitful. Your patience and your thoughtful, sensitive criticisms taught me to listen to the ideas of others without feeling threatened. You taught me that "others" often have important and valuable questions, thoughts, ideas and insights that may serve to enhance my work. Thank you for suggesting and encouraging me to seek publication for *A Moral Emergency*. If you hadn't suggested it, and even "pushed" me a little, I'm sure this manuscript would be neatly filed away, in my blue metal filing cabinet, along with all my other Divinity School papers.

J. Giles Milhaven, Professor of Religious Studies
Brown University
Providence, Rhode Island

Thank you Giles, for treating me as a colleague and friend, even while I was "still a student." Your respect for my knowledge, which was not yet accompanied by an "official" degree, gave me confidence. Thank you for your distinct and careful comments regarding this manuscript. Your attention to detail helped me to clarify my thinking. Thank you, also, for providing me with the opportunity to talk with your students at Brown University about the connections between child sexual abuse and anger. It was an enlightening, empowering experience . . . and *now more people know!*

Robert Heyer, Editor-in-Chief
Sheed & Ward
Kansas City, Missouri

Thank you Bob, for hearing about the issue of child sexual abuse, and for taking a chance on publishing a book on a topic that many people refer to as a "negative" social issue. They are not always the best sellers, and consequently not the most lucrative investments for publishers. Thank you for your suggestions which transformed this manuscript from an academic thesis into a more creative and interesting project for me, and a more comprehensive handbook for religious leaders. Bob, on behalf of the victims and the survivors of child sexual abuse—past, present and future—I say thank you for making an effort to bring this issue, this devastating pain, out into the open within the religious communities in America.

# *Foreword*

I resist this book still.

I first read Jade Angelica's manuscript a year ago when my class and I read it, wrote on it, and discussed it for several hours with the author herself. Now, invited to write this foreword, I have read the final, further developed manuscript. From my first reading on, I keep saying: "Yes!" "Yes!" "Absolutely!" "We must know this!" "We must do something!"

In my reading, I note that at places I pause and ponder. Mainly when I think things like, "Isn't that too simplistic?", or, "Does this really follow?," or, "Is that completely practical?" "What does this word mean?," "But what if ____?" In brief, in reading this book, I find that I pause mainly to question critically on minor, academic points. But while these queries have, I think, some validity, it interests me to note that I have not followed them up. I have not put any of these questions to Jade; nor have I myself made an effort to answer them.

Instead, I have noticed, upon reflection, that there are two places in the book at which I never pause. Quickly I have read through the numerous personal accounts by victims of child sexual abuse. Never have I read them slowly, openly and freely. Never attentively, letting them sink into me word by word. Similarly, I have never read slowly, paused and pondered the factual statistics and the picture they record. In both instances—the stories and the statistics—I felt an inner pressure, a visceral tensing, pressing my eyes to hasten on, urging my attention to move to the next section. Invariably, I followed that pressure.

But what would happen if I resisted this hastening pressure? If I made myself pause and read slowly what happened, detail by detail, what "Stephen" tells me? what "Gayle" describes? what "Annamarie" recounts? What if I took time to imagine a fully human story behind each statistical number? What if I let myself imagine what these statistics might represent—as I watch children playing, as I watch my grandson, Lewie, and my granddaughter, Stephanie, playing in my backyard?

What will it do to me if the pain of some victims, whether still children or now adults, penetrates me? If I identify for even a minute with their hope struggling with despair? If I just listen to them for a while as I try hard not to defend myself? I am afraid. But, like Lewie and Stephanie when they are in trouble, so, too, individuals who have been "sexually abused by people they know and trust and love" face me silently—grief, fear and desire on their faces.

I have spent time reflecting on Jade's practical conclusions, particularly the proposals she makes towards the end of the book. I support them. I admire them as I do the whole book. I tell my friends about the book and recommend it to them strongly. And I will use the book again this semester in my course.

I will read the book again. I will read the personal stories more slowly. And the statistics. The whole book, I know, will then move me closer to these children, or these adults who were once these children. I don't expect to end up with new words and concepts. The question is: how much will it change my life? For them and for me?

J. Giles Milhaven

# *Preface*

People often ask me about the work I'm doing. They wonder . . . why I'm doing it . . . Is it depressing and discouraging . . . Do I feel helpless and hopeless?

I can't deny that hearing about the details of the sexual abuse of children from the victims and the survivors is sickening and heartbreaking. But I have been mobilized into action by the horrible realities of this issue, in spite of any feelings of depression I might have. I have been energized by the positive responses and encouragement I have received from those working in the field and those now familiar—from my work—with the issue.

There's a simple answer to WHY I'm doing this work. Now I know—in quantities and detailed descriptions—about the sexual abuse of children in America. Haunting memories of past atrocities insist upon my attention to present atrocities.

In the spring of 1991 I watched "Gabriel's Fire," a detective show on television. The main character in the mystery was an elderly Jewish man who was depressed, angry, sullen and solitary. When the unmistakable brand on his forearm was revealed, the other television characters—and I—instantly understood, without any explanation, the details of his tortuous internment in a Nazi concentration camp. His otherwise antisocial behaviors became acceptable and somehow admirable. The television characters and I forgave the man's rudeness and embraced him completely and compassionately in his struggle. This all happened without even one spoken word. The brand on his forearm said it all.

In 1979 I saw a television documentary on the Holocaust, and was horrified by the images which were eternally burned into my consciousness through my eyes. Those images haunted me day and night. Finally, in despair, I called my mother, who, in the early 1940s, had been a young wife and mother. I told her of the distress I was experiencing from bearing witness to the horrors of the Holocaust. Then I asked her, "Why did you let this happen, Mom? Why didn't you do something? Why didn't America do something?" Her reply was sincere. She said softly, "Honey, we didn't know."

And it was true—then. But now we do know. And there are agencies and documentaries and branded concentration camp survivors making sure we never forget. And rightly so. This universal outrage at the atrocity of the Holocaust helps to ensure that such a horror will not happen again to the Jewish people.

The trauma of child sexual abuse victims and survivors, the trauma of concentration camp victims and survivors, and the trauma of combat veterans is similar simply because it is all trauma. But since there are no brands or missing limbs, the anguish, anger, depression and loss resulting from the trauma of child sexual abuse are usually not recognized or embraced. For survivors of child sexual abuse there is not yet acknowledged, universal outrage, nor is there any assurance that the atrocity will not happen again. Mostly, tragically, there is just denial. But now that I *know* about child sexual abuse, I am motivated to do what I can to stop any further destruction of small, innocent, vulnerable people.

The answer to WHY I have chosen to invite religious communities to join me in learning about child sexual abuse and in doing what we can to stop this abuse is more complex. I've known about child sexual abuse for a number of years. And I've always known that I would do "something" about it. But what that something would be wasn't always so clear.

At first I was convinced that punishment of the abusers was the one and only answer. Therefore, an internship at the Child Abuse Prosecution Unit of the local district attorney's office seemed the perfect placement for me: here was an entire office whose sole focus was to punish people! I searched my divinity school textbooks for biblical and ethical justifications for punishment and righteous anger.

But as I learned about the justice system, the social service agencies, and the realities of the lifetime healing process of the victims of child sexual abuse, a new understanding began to dawn. I realized that neither the solution, nor even the seeds of the remedy, for this epidemic would be found in the justice system. I continue to believe that people who sexually abuse children should be held accountable and punished, and I applaud the justice system for its efforts; however, I am now convinced that the solution to the problem of child sexual abuse lies in widespread attitudinal changes regarding the position and treatment of children in our homes and in our communities. The solution lies in spiritual and psychological healing of the damaged souls and hearts of the millions of victims and survivors and abusers. The solution lies in adult abusers being responsible and saying "no" to their sexual impulses toward children.

"Social morality is a corollary of personal morality . . . and the strength of personal morality does not come from law but from a spiritual revival."[1] These are the words of a Unitarian minister, Francis Greenwood Peabody. In 1904 Peabody, a professor at Harvard, delivered the Lyman Beecher lectures at Yale. This series of eight lectures was entitled "Jesus and the Christian Character." Into these lectures, Peabody introduced the element of "moral obligation," insisting that the whole duty of humanity "is to descend with the grace of God to the help of humans."[2]

And so I have turned to the religious communities, sharing with them the knowledge I have about the moral emergency of child sexual abuse. I believe that the religious communities possess the opportunity and the power to *name* the atrocity of child sexual abuse, to begin *dismantling the denial*, to *offer solace* to the victims and survivors, to *insist upon accountability* from the abusers, and *to plant the seeds of universal outrage*. I also believe that the religious communities are morally obligated to do so. "We didn't know" can no longer be accepted as an innocent excuse for not protecting our children.

# Introduction

*A Moral Emergency* is the culmination of years of academic and empirical research, from a multi-disciplinary perspective, concerning various aspects of the issue of child sexual abuse. Through my observations and research, I have concluded that the religious communities in the United States truly need to begin focusing on the issue of child sexual abuse in a deliberate and concentrated way. *A Moral Emergency*, a comprehensive, introductory handbook for religious leaders, is offered as a way to begin. It both informs people about the problem of child sexual abuse and invites them to become a part of the solution.

Chapters 1 - 3 clearly define the problem of child sexual abuse within our society. Chapter 4 is a detailed history of child sexual abuse, with a primarily religious focus. Chapter 5 provides the results of a telephone survey of eight religious denominations which was conducted in the spring of 1991 in an attempt to determine how religious communities were responding to the emergency of child sexual abuse. As this book was being revised in the fall of 1992, some follow-up information was added. Chapter 6 challenges religious leaders to invite their communities to "hear" about the issue of child sexual abuse and to "act." An outline for a program for prophetic ministry is offered, suggesting a variety of actions religious communities can realistically take toward stopping the sexual abuse of children. In a time when too many people feel utterly helpless about effecting change regarding social problems, the proposed program will provide challenges as well as hope for healing. Chapter 7 offers a glimpse at the healing and a glimmer of hope.

Each chapter, and each section within Chapter 3, begins with personal accounts of adult survivors of child sexual abuse. These accounts have been selected carefully with the intention of setting the tone for the information which follows. The accounts were either reprinted with permission from previously published materials or previously broadcast programs, or provided to me directly by survivors for use in this book. Although only first names identify the accounts, the names have been respectfully changed as requested by individual survivors.

Although the survey data was gathered from Christian Churches and the Unitarian Universalist Association of Congregations, the phrase "religious community" has been used instead of "church" throughout *A Moral Emergency*, except when referring to a specific organization. The phrase has been used deliberately with the intent of acknowledging the growing cultural and religious diversity in America, and inviting churches, synagogues, mosques, temples, etc. to be included in the movement to hear about child sexual abuse.

In recent months, the sexual abuse of children by members of the Christian clergy has received enormous amounts of media attention and has been met by public outcry. This type of child sexual abuse is addressed only very briefly in *A Moral Emergency*. This brief treatment of clergy abuse in no way seeks to diminish the importance of that issue. I do, however, want to remain firm about not blurring the two issues. The topic of "clergy abuse" is about the *abuser*. *A Moral Emergency* is about the *abused*. Child victims and adult survivors of child sexual abuse need our attention and concern, regardless of who abused them, be it priest, relative or stranger.

Since I have had the pleasure and the challenge of living, working and studying in the Greater Boston area for the past 14 years, much of the information and many of the examples in *A Moral Emergency* are drawn from local sources. Hopefully, a predominantly Massachusetts "flavor" will not detract from the message of the book, especially since there is nothing unique to Massachusetts regarding child sexual abuse. The advantages of the regional information are the accuracy and relevance. I analyzed the raw statistics myself. I know what and who each number represents, and have included some of this empirical data in Chapter 2 and Appendix 2. I am grateful to Kellie Pini of the Middlesex County District Attorney's Office for her willingness to help me understand and analyze the statistics she so competently manages.

What is happening in Massachusetts is happening all across the country. However, as I've documented in Chapter 2 and Appendix 2, it is difficult, at best, to gather specific, detailed data about child sexual abuse on a national scale. Perhaps after reading *A Moral Emergency*, religious leaders will be inspired to seek empirical information from their local district attorneys' offices or their state social services agencies, and send it to me in care of Sheed & Ward. People who are working to protect our children need to have accurate, detailed information from every county in every state. We need to know more about this emergency. We have a right to know. "Ask and it will be given you, search and you will find, knock and the door will be opened for you." (NRSV Luke 11:5-8)

The more we know, the more we can help.

# CHAPTER ONE

# The Prosecutor and the Ethicist: A Metaphor for Society's Response to Child Sexual Abuse

People don't recognize violence as violence
because it has become a way of life.
—Claudia Black, PhD., *Sound of Silence*

## Steve

### *"To Protect the Children"*

I'm a businessman.  I own my own business that employs
a lot of people and does quite a bit of business.  I was a very
successful kid.  I was captain of the football team and president
of my high school class.  I went to Harvard.  So from every
possible measure, including my own basic sense of satisfaction,
I was doing just fine.

But there was this one little idiosyncrasy, which was this
guy who was a very close family friend, who had been a friend
of my father's from as far back as World War II.  He had lived
around the country, basically by coincidence, in areas similar to
where we had lived.  He was, in fact, an abuser, a sexual
abuser of little kids, which my parents knew.  But they were
sticking with him as a friend.  What they didn't know was that
I was one of the little kids who was on the program.

I don't know when it began.  I'm not sure if my memory
can still dredge certain things out of the mire.  There was always a kind of overlay of this guy's imposition on my privacy
and private parts, and my constantly having to fight the guy
off in the context of my family's embracing him.

1

There were a couple of instances where there were explicit sexual activities that took place, but it was more that when he would come over to our house, which was frequently, early in the morning, he would be sent upstairs to wake us up and there would be hands crawling under my covers trying to reach me. And that's going on in this environment of "This guy's a wonderful guy."

The message that I got was that somehow my being sexually subordinated to this guy was approved by my parents, which it clearly wasn't—overtly, but that's what I picked up. What I picked up was that this was my proper role. This was what I was supposed to be doing.

I think society needs to respond aggressively to protect the children and to make sure the right message is given to the children. If these things are treated lightly, then the absolute wrong message is given to us, that is, that there wasn't any big deal. So what's the problem? What are you complaining about?[1] ❖

## Catherine

### "Just to Survive"

Chip is a five-year-old child who hates to wear socks, but who loves cartoons and cookies made with M&M's. Chip's aversion for socks is only one connection between Kim and Chip. Kim's father and brother used to take turns raping her with a sock covering their penises. So Kim created Chip and dozens of other personalities just to survive.

Faith must wear long "evening gloves" of pressure wrap to contain the scars which cover her hands and arms. Her father and several of his drunken cronies tied her to a tree and raped her. Then they set the tree on fire. She escaped only when the ropes around her wrists had burnt off. Faith must have a staff member with her at all times, to protect her from herself, just to survive.

The sexual abuse that I survived seems trivial when compared with the abuse that Kim and Faith had to endure. My abuser didn't practice ritual abuse, he didn't rape me, or try to murder me. My abuser, my father, used to masturbate over me while I pretended to be sleeping and grab my breasts when I tried to pass him in the hallway. I don't have 40-something personalities, and I don't wear pressure gloves, but I have suffered, and I do have scars. I believe that I will always suffer, just as I will always have scars. Nothing is going to make it go away. It is a part of me.

As long as the world remains as it is, and as long as adults continue to molest children, the scars will remain a part of all of us. But we must try to make it easier to live with it while we must. We must allow the Kims and Faiths to cry out, to roar, so that they may be heard, and so that they may heal themselves.[2] ❖

## The Prosecutor and the Ethicist

I interviewed them both, in that order, on the very same day, one right after the other. Perhaps the order and the timing of the interviews accentuated the differences I experienced—*on that day*—in their approaches to the issue of child sexual abuse. It was more than a year later before I began to understand how their differences had similarities, and how their points and conclusions resembled one another's, but were reached from completely different paths.

I expected the prosecutor to be business-like, factual and somewhat dispassionate as we discussed the legal aspects of child sexual abuse. I was, therefore, surprised to encounter a man who was, yes, business-like and factual, but also impassioned about the need to protect children. He had spent time with the tiny victims of child sexual abuse. He had heard and seen the details of their abuse and the devastating effects; he had embraced their pain, and had watched them struggle through the frightening court system—which, he added, in itself is enough to terrify even the most confident adult. The prosecutor had spent much time in contemplation regarding the sexual abuse of children, and had concluded that no one working with child victims of abuse of any kind could help but become emotionally involved.

He spoke about "right" and "wrong," returning several time to stress this subject. He suggested that "we all"—meaning the justice system, the social service agencies, the schools, the religious communities, the families, the whole of society—

need to do a better job of helping people to understand that the sexual abuse of children is WRONG.

He suggested that forceful prosecution of child sex offenders and mandatory, lengthy jail sentences could create "awareness" between right and wrong. And this is what the justice system can do. He believes it is his responsibility as prosecutor to bring wrong behaviors to the attention of the public, and to ensure that there are consequences for those wrong behaviors. However, he also understands that the justice system cannot single-handedly solve the problem of child sexual abuse in American society; the justice system cannot be expected to solve this problem. But, he added, the justice system can prosecute—*it is going to prosecute*—these crimes against children.

We talked about other methods of communicating "This is wrong!" to society. The prosecutor thought that the power of advertising could be persuasive; that perhaps—as some have suggested and as some have tried—ads on billboards and radio and television commercials, clearly stating "This is wrong," could make an impression on people. Prevention programs in schools and religious communities could also help. Again he returned to "wrong," stressing the need for awareness, however it could be accomplished. Awareness versus the "out of sight, out of mind" attitude which now pervades in society. He had seen lives being ruined, lives being sacrificed. How could anyone just let this situation "be"?

And then the prosecutor became a bit of a philosopher. He talked about how we treat one another in our society, especially children. Again, back to right and wrong. He believes that we've *all* lost sight—in many ways—of what's right and what's wrong. Lost sight? Or closed our eyes? Somewhere, he wasn't sure exactly where, but somewhere, the prosecutor believes that "we have lost our way." We're influenced, today, by things other than morality. It seemed to him that material things were more important than basic right and wrong. Warped values. He repeated it. A warped sense of values.

The prosecutor closed our discussion by talking about the Child Abuse Reporting Law. This law *forces* people who work with children in professional capacities to report suspected or actual child abuse to the social service and/or legal authorities. This law, he said, forces people to "think" about the issue. And thus he concluded: since *any* abuse of children is so clearly

WRONG, if people thought about it, even for a minute, no one would so much as put a hand on a child.

These words of the prosecutor were still an echo in my mind as I sat in the ethicist's office. We had a difficult time, the ethicist and I, getting to the point of discussing child sexual abuse and how religious communities and society could make a difference. He began talking about his commitment to "nurturance." The issue of child sexual abuse didn't seem to compute compatibly with the ethicist's theory of nurturance. And as he continued to talk, the echo of the prosecutor's final words became combined with the words the ethicist was speaking. The ethicist frankly could not believe that anyone could or would raise a hand to a child. Obviously, he had thought about it. He talked on about his grandson, about the small boy's desire for affection and cuddling, about how the child would climb up onto his grandpa's lap requesting hugs and kisses. How could anyone exploit a child's desire for affection? How could anyone raise a hand to a child?

For a moment, my consciousness was distracted from what the ethicist was saying. And for that moment I envisioned us—the prosecutor, the ethicist and me—as comrades in battle, in the jungle or in the desert. I was the sergeant coming fresh from the battlefield, where I had fought side by side with the prosecutor "general," to this meeting with the ethicist "general." My clothes and hands were still damp with the blood of the casualties. The dirt on my face was streaked with tears. The ethicist general was observing and directing this war from the clean, air-conditioned, efficient safety of his office at command control, distant and removed from the mess of blood and destruction. The ethicist general spoke in theories which were common knowledge and written about at length in all of the manuals. It was clearly difficult for him to face the reality of the issue I represented. He was troubled. I had punctured his theories. He spoke so adoringly of his grandson. We were both grateful, I think, that this boy was protected from the battle. I could see the boy's tiny hand snugly engulfed by his grandpa's large one as the ethicist general talked about teaching the boy to safely cross the road. There was clearly no abuse here, no wrong. Only love. Vulnerable love. The love and concern for his grandson beamed brightly through the ethicist general's eyes and words and heart. This is the way it should be. But—for too many children—it's not the way it is. Theory belies practice.

I tried to gently bring the conversation back to the reality of the battlefield and the wounded. I did this knowing it was my mission to discuss child sexual abuse with this renowned ethicist, but I felt a bit guilty because I realized I was shattering his innocence. This was not a concern with the prosecutor. His innocence had been shattered years ago, along with the innocence of the first child victim he had encountered.

The ethicist brought up the subject of pornography, believing this was a contributing factor to the breakdown of moral behavior within our society. Trying to keep the discussion focused on the subject of child sexual abuse, I asked him if he knew that some of the soft-pornography magazines, which are now a totally sanctioned part of American culture, contain cartoons depicting and glorifying sex with children. The ethicist was shocked. It showed. He couldn't imagine this. Surely, he said, if presented with such an image he would totally repress it. I wondered how the ethicist would react to the piece of pornographic evidence of violent child sexual abuse I had seen at the prosecutor's office. I glanced at this photograph for no longer than 2 or 3 seconds because that's all my stomach could tolerate. But those 2 or 3 seconds horrified my consciousness and forever changed my life. I wondered how the ethicist would react to such an image. Again, I felt concern for his innocence. What right did I have to try to destroy it as he struggled to maintain it?

But the ethicist's comment about repressing an image too horrifying to contain in the conscious mind caused me to wonder just how often we as a society see things or hear things or experience things that we don't pay attention to, *can't* pay attention to. The prosecutor referenced the Child Abuse Reporting Law which *forces* people, using the threat of prosecution for not reporting, to report child abuse. Due to this reporting law, the number of cases of child sexual abuse reported to the prosecutor's office rose dramatically from 91 in 1983 to 204 in 1984 to 715 in 1990.[3] Do we see and respond to the issue of child sexual abuse only when we are forced to? Does the threat of prosecution for failure to report improve our eyesight? Does it increase our moral courage?

The ethicist spoke at length of moral courage. It was the subject he kept returning to throughout our conversation. Our society is founded on the moral custom of privacy and the rights of people to do "whatever they want" in their own homes. And even when "whatever they want" involves sexually abusing children, the ethicist believes it will take a person with great moral courage to "knock on the door" of a private home and interrupt that behavior. Then the ethicist asked the same question the prosecutor asked. How have we come to this point? After all, we're all in this life, this world—together. But we're not in each other's homes—together. Each person has his or her own family, and other people are "outsiders." The message to outsiders is "stay out."

It takes moral courage to risk getting involved with children's rights, because most children "belong" to someone else. But all people have rights, and we all have responsibilities to one another; only then, according to the ethicist, do our rights have a chance to flourish. But no child has any rights unless someone enforces them . . . someone of moral courage.

The ethicist kept pondering "moral courage," wondering if he—or I—could guarantee that we would go against the moral custom of privacy and do what was necessary to protect the children. My consciousness drifted off again, this time into my memory. I'll never forget that night. I had been visiting married friends who were the parents of two children. After leaving their home, I realized I had forgotten something and I returned. Their son, who was 9 at the time, had disobeyed and gone back outside to play. His father was furious. I stood inside the house, at the doorway. The boy was outside the house, at the doorway. His mother was reprimanding him. His father saw the boy, became enraged and pushed past me, out the door. The boy cowered on the porch, covered his face with his arms and screamed, "No. Don't hit me. Please don't hit me." The father—6' 2" tall, weighing 250 pounds—grabbed the scrawny boy, launching him into the air, it seemed. The boy flew past me into the house, and amidst the screams of the child, father and son disappeared from my view. I stood frozen to the spot at the doorway, saying nothing about the scene I had just witnessed. I said goodnight to the boy's mother and I left. For days, weeks, months, I wondered if I should report what I had seen to the Department of Social Services. I still wonder. But the moral custom of privacy, fueled by my cowardice, won out. I convinced myself that this was not my business, and maybe that it wasn't even abuse. I didn't want to insult my friends or jeopardize our friendship. The child was the sacrifice. Returning from this memory, I looked up at the ethicist and quietly answered him. "No, I can't guarantee that I will do whatever is necessary to protect the children."

The ethicist turned his focus to right and wrong. Like the prosecutor, he believes we need to "awaken" the sense of right and wrong in society. But he did not focus on "wrong." He focused on "right." He focused on rebuilding community and repairing relationships. A true ethicist, his beliefs were rooted firmly in the affirmation that goodness is more powerful than evil. He felt that the righteous indignation I expressed regarding child sexual abuse would alienate the decent people rather than rally them to support the cause. He urged me to shift my emotional energy to healing instead of punishment.

I wanted to be convinced by his convictions, but like the prosecutor, I had seen and heard the accounts of the child victims. I had witnessed their pain. Their blood had been splattered on me and I would never be the same. Yes, I was indignant about this abuse. But I was moved to a different emotional level by my conversation with the ethicist. His adoration of his grandchild, of all children, was precious and endearing. What a kind, upstanding man. His love and concern for humanity was inspiring. His *belief* in humanity was inspiring.

But when I left him, the inspiration I felt was mixed with a sadness that went deep into my soul. I had heard the ethicist's message about love and healing, but had he heard how serious the issue of child sexual abuse actually is in our society? Immersed in his invested interest in how things "should be," I feared that he wouldn't notice and be attentive to how things "are." His theoretical, philosophical conclusion of "goodness prevails" seemed to have no relevance to my questions regarding child sexual abuse, no relevance to the child victims. How could I return to these raped and assaulted children and tell them "goodness prevails"?

These two interviews took place—geographically—just a few miles apart, but philosophically they were worlds apart. The prosecutor focused on accountability and punishment. His role in preventing crimes against children is to convince people that certain behaviors are "wrong." The ethicist focused on love and healing. His role is to teach people what is "right," to help people grapple with difficult moral problems, in theory, and reach conclusions that morally benefit humankind, in theory. The prosecutor's practical experience translated more realistically into theory than did the ethicist's theoretical experience translate into practice. In fact, it seemed that when confronted with the issue of child sexual abuse, the theoretical approach was rendered practically powerless in the face of the horrifying reality.

By preaching God's love and acceptance of all, including sinners and criminals, religious communities have historically followed the philosophy of the ethicist. There has not been a strong focus on "wrong," especially regarding the treatment of children. People have learned that they will be forgiven by a benevolent God who loves them, even when they do wrong. After all, we are only human! However, forgiven—by God and/or the victims—or not, the prosecutor still insists that all human beings who abuse others be held accountable for their actions. He is preaching "consequences." Religious communities have focused on forgiving, leaving "earthly" accountability to the justice system. However, this delegation of power has not been effective in deterring crimes against children. On its own, each approach is limited in its effectiveness. But together? Perhaps some blend of accountability and love, some blend of prosecutor and ethicist could be the beginnings of a solution to the problem of child sexual abuse.

As I thought back over my interviews with the prosecutor and the ethicist, I was surprised that they had reached similar conclusions: A widespread change in attitude regarding children is imperative. Although their methods of awakening people differed, they agreed that awakening people to an awareness of right and wrong regarding the treatment of children is most imperative. And finally, they agreed that the only true way to deal with the issue of child sexual abuse is to get at the underlying cause. And they agreed on the cause: we, as human beings living in the world community, do not love and respect each other—especially the children—enough.

A month after the interview, my fears about the ethicist not hearing about child sexual abuse vanished. I received a note from him which was short but empowering. It said simply, "I have benefited from our discussion. Thank you." There was no question about it; he had heard, and he would never be the same. The ethicist is now busy uncovering some new pieces of information in his ethics "manuals"; information regarding children and sexual abuse that previously was buried because his eyes did not yet know what to search for. The ethicist's eyes were opened; his innocence was lost.[4]

# CHAPTER TWO

# *Child Sexual Abuse in Perspective: Available Data and Statistics*

After 125 years of discarded enlightenment, we still act as if victims are freaks and as if it is a virtue to be ignorant of sexual victimization. We pretend nobody is involved, even though the veterans may outnumber the recruits.
—Roland C. Summit, M.D., *Hidden Victims, Hidden Pain*

## Susan

### *"A Casualty of Life"*

My life story does not begin happily, for I am a survivor of childhood incest and abuse. I was sexually abused by my father for more than 13 years, and beaten, ridiculed and terrorized by my alcoholic mother throughout my life. My home life was abusive in ways that many children do not survive. Some become casualties by suicide, but most are casualties to alcoholism, drug addiction, self-abuse, prostitution, compulsive and abusive behaviors and relationships, depression, despair, and pervasive fear.

I cannot deny or erase my past, and as a result of it I carry a permanent scar. I am one of the casualties. But unlike the soldiers of war or victims of accidents or physical handicaps who have suffered visible damage, eyes cannot see what I have lost. Nonetheless, I have lost things of great importance. I have lost my childhood, my innocence, my self-esteem. I have lost the ability to trust and the capacity to love. I have lost my family. I was betrayed, and then left alone to heal a wound I didn't even know I had.[1] ❖

## Annamarie

### *"My life wasn't like the Beaver's"*

It's very difficult for me to talk about my life without detaching myself, so the following description will seem cold or flat. It's easier to write about it.

I am the oldest daughter of a middle class European-descended family. I have one older brother. My name is Annamarie and my family life was far different from that of Beaver Cleaver. As far back as I can remember, I was sexually abused by my maternal grandfather, and at the age of 11 my brother started to use me as his learning tool for sex. I do not remember a lot of the details of my grandfather's abuse because he used to get me drunk to abuse me, although this did serve the purpose of keeping me numb until I was about 21. I sobered up then and started dealing with my past.

The scattered memories of my grandfather's abuse never left my side. In fact when I think about it, I still get a sickened feeling and a choking feeling as my head flashes the memory of gagging on his tongue as it is deep in my mouth. I also still gag on the hair as I try to get it out of my mouth. I sometimes feel thankful for the numbing agent that he let me pick out. I am not sure how long the abuse lasted, and I do remember talking to my auntie Gerry and telling her that I couldn't get grandpa to stop "kissing" me. He was always on me when we were alone. She said it was because he loved me so much, and then she talked with him about it. I thought it would be over since I heard her tell him that he was only allowed to kiss me two times a day, once in the morning and once before bed. I thought I was saved, but that only lasted for a few days, and then I lost all hope, because he didn't listen to the adult. I felt that nothing could or would stop him.

Since I was raised in a traditional European household, I was not allowed to speak my mind, and this halted the situation even more. By the time my brother started to abuse me, I was so used to doing what I was told, and that males had absolute authority, I just lived with that was the way my life was going to be. The abusive relationship with my brother ended when I got pregnant at the age of 13 and had an abortion.

To this day I have problems with close relationships. I also have problems with large, dirty (unclean) men. And even though I tried to detach myself while I write this, I still feel saddened and enraged by this. Talking about this and wanting to get well has caused a complete separation from the rest of my family because of denial. The sad part is that I know of others that my grandfather has sexually abused and I can't even discuss it with them.[2] ❖

## Child Sexual Abuse in Perspective

Between January 15 and February 27, 1991, the collective eyes and ears of America were focused on the television news, watching and listening anxiously for updates on the war in the Persian Gulf. The yellow ribbons which decorated tree trunks and telephone poles, coat lapels, car radio antennas, porch railings, shop windows, billboards, and the doors of homes, churches and synagogues represented the country's solidarity with the Allied hostages and troops in Saudi Arabia. People were organized, mobilized and marching in the streets, giving voice—and action—to their support for the troops, or to their protests against the violence of war. Candlelight vigils, American flags and "The Battle Hymn of the Republic" tugged on the heartstrings of America. In religious communities across the country, prayers for peace in the Middle East were raised to the heavens. There was, and always is, great and justifiable concern for our brothers and sisters who face the inevitable dangers of war. 60,000 American men and women lost their lives in Vietnam[3]; more American lives were threatened in the desert.

During 1990, 150 people were murdered in the troubled neighborhoods of Boston.[4] City officials, police officers, religious leaders, and concerned citizens meet regularly, seeking solutions to this continuing and escalating violence. People are afraid. In religious communities throughout the metropolitan area, prayers for peace on the streets of Boston are raised to the heavens. There is great and justifiable concern about the violence on the city streets, and it has become a "pressing issue" because "the murder rate is soaring."[5]

My intent is not to minimize these tragedies of war and violence in the cities, but to put them in perspective. In 1986 the American Humane Association collected data on child sexual abuse, and according to their information, over 140,000 reports of child sexual abuse are filed each year in the United States. It is generally recognized by professionals that reported cases of child sexual abuse represent a "mere fraction" of the actual cases of child sexual abuse occurring in America.[6] Two sources, *Victims No More*, by Mike Lew and *About Sexual Abuse*, the Unitarian Universalist religious education curriculum, both indicated that over 500,000 children are sexually abused each year in the United States, although neither provided documentation for this number. A 1985 Policy Statement from the Big Brother Association of Boston indicated that the estimated number of children who are sexually assaulted in the United States each year could be as high as 1,000,000. Again, no documentation accompanied this estimate. Perhaps this discrepancy in estimates can be attributed to the difference between prosecuted cases, reported cases, and the unknown number of children who do not tell, plus the number who do not remember. A recent longitudinal study of documented female victims of child sexual abuse found that "38% of the women were amnesic for the abuse or chose not to report it . . . 17 years later."[7]

It is also generally acknowledged that gathering accurate national statistics regarding the cases of child sexual abuse is, at this time, *impossible*. One rape crisis professional in Seattle defined the difficulty as "the Black Hole of Bureaucracy."[8] Many child protective workers from a variety of states literally laughed at my request for statistics on child sexual abuse. Their laughter was an expression of frustration for they, too, were trying to collect this information. A researcher at The National Resource Center on Child Sexual Abuse in Huntsville, Alabama calmly explained that the information just *does not exist*. And the reason IS bureaucracy! At the current time there is no standard way of compiling and tabulating data from the 50 states. Social service and law enforcement agencies—in each state—have diverse methods of reporting as well as collecting data. And to complicate the situation even more, different states have different laws, as well as different legal definitions of "child" and "abuse."

And so, "estimation" is totally what our statistical data consists of in 1992 regarding the number of children sexually abused each year in the United States. And yet, because some states do compile and maintain detailed statistics, perhaps the estimations can be meaningful. For example, in 1991, in the state of Washington there were 75,476 reports of child maltreatment, involving 62,000 child victims, reported to child protective services. 14,338 of those reports involved child sexual abuse.[9] Not all states separate the reports of child maltreatment by "type" as standard procedure, which is why there is no firm national data on child sexual abuse reports. However, if the Washington reports of 14,338 can be considered *average* among the 50 states—which is a reasonable consideration since the number of child sexual abuse reports in California in 1991 was 102,200[10]—and the number of their reports is multiplied by 50, we can estimate that the number of cases of child sexual abuse reported to social service agencies in the United States in 1991 was over 700,000.

The Commonwealth of Massachusetts does not separate the child abuse reports by type of maltreatment; however their data, broken down in another way, is also informative. In 1991, 88,748 reports of child abuse were filed with the Department of Social Services. 28,048 cases were investigated and confirmed. 2,858 children were so severely abused that their cases were considered of a criminal nature and were referred to the district attorneys' offices.[11] The detailed data compiled in Middlesex County indicates that routinely 95% of the cases of child abuse referred to district attorneys' offices in Massachusetts involve sexual abuse.[12] If Middlesex county can be considered an average county in an average state, we can estimate that 95% of the cases referred to district attorneys' offices involve sexual abuse of a criminal nature. 95% of 2858 is 2715. If the Massachusetts data is multiplied by the 50 states, it can be estimated that 135,750 cases of child sexual abuse reach the criminal justice system in the United States each year.

But there is another way of estimating the number of victims. According to renowned researcher David Finkelhor, estimates regarding the incidence of child sexual abuse are more commonly, more accurately done by percentages based on random sample studies. For example, in 1984, Finkelhor reviewed all prior studies on the sexual abuse of boys under the age of 13 and concluded the "true prevalence figure" might be between 2.5% and 5%. Assuming the lowest rate, 2.5%, 550,000 of the 20 million boys in that age group in the United States have been sexually abused. Therefore, approximately 46,000 new victimizations of boys under the age of 13 would occur each year.[13]

Because the sexual abuse of children is "a crime too cruel for mind and memory to face,"[14] many people doubt and dismiss the estimated statistics. And it is far easier to dismiss the statistics than to believe them. But the evidence is rising. And although the statistics are estimated, they are startling and we must believe them.

These startling statistics are not particularly "news." In 1953, Alfred Kinsey, zoology professor from Indiana University, published the results of his survey about female sexuality. His sample included more than 4000 white, middle-class, educated, urban women. One in four participants in the study reported having sexual contact with an adult male or being approached by a man—or men—for sex before the age of 12. Most of the girls reported that they knew their assailants.[15] In 1983, Diana Russell conducted a study using a more random sample and discovered that 38% of those responding had sexual contact with an adult male during childhood.[16] A national survey done by David Finkelhor in 1985 indicated that 27% of women and 16% of men had been sexually abused as children.[17]

The random sample studies which have attempted to document the sexual abuse of children have not been consistent in their definitions of "sexual abuse." In the Kinsey study, non-contact types of offenses, such as indecent exposure, were included.[18] The Finkelhor study required actual physical contact in its definition of sexual abuse. This contact ranged from sexual touching and fondling to rape.[19]

But *statistics*, no matter how startling, are sterile and clinical. They distance us from the realities they represent. What IS sexual abuse? One answer can be provided through the justice system. In the Commonwealth of Massachusetts, the sexual abuse of children falls into the following legally-defined categories: exploitation (which includes but is not limited to pornography), indecent exposure, forcible rape, rape, sexual assault and battery, sexual assault with the intent to rape, and unspecified sexual assault. The definitions and distinctions are very clear. Any sexual touching of a child, with or without the clothes on of either victim or perpetrator, or any sexual invasion or interaction with a child under the age of 16 is considered criminal behavior. Technically, an assault can be any approach or action that puts someone in fear. Rape is defined as penetration of any orifice, with any object or body part, and includes oral, vaginal or anal intercourse.[20]

WHO do the statistics represent? They represent the children—our children—our future. They represent the most vulnerable citizens of our nation. And so we don't get caught up in the statistics and forget who they represent, two charts of "statistics" reduced down to the level of the individual child victim have been explicated and included as reference. The charts represent the children who were sexually abused in Middlesex County, Massachusetts in 1990. I analyzed the raw data provided by the district attorney's office myself. The tabulations were done by hand.

In 1990, 767 cases of child abuse were referred to the Middlesex County District Attorney's Office by the Department of Social Services, local or state police departments, or concerned citizens for investigation. As indicated by *CHART #1*, 685 children were sexually abused; 30 children were both sexually and physically abused; 45 children were physically abused, including 13 children who died from their injuries. *CHART #2* explicates the various types of child sexual abuse by charge. In the case of multiple charges, only the "lead charge," which is the most heinous as determined by the district attorney, was tabulated. As indicated by *CHART #2*, 200 children under the age of 14 were indecently assaulted; 43 children between the ages of 14 and 16 were indecently assaulted; 360 children were raped; 9 children were assaulted with the intent to rape; 96 children were sexually assaulted; 6 children were photographed in sexually explicit ways; 1 child was subjected to indecent exposure.

*CHARTS #1* AND #2 were included with the intent of providing a "visual" exhibit; however, they became much, much more for me. As I was going through the hundreds of forms provided to me by the district attorney's office—counting and recounting with focused and intent determination—I suddenly was awakened, and I realized what I was doing. It occurred to me that each mark I made on the page was more than a "statistic." Each mark represented a child—a small human being. I looked at the mark I had just made on the paper; I looked at the form to see "what" the mark on the paper represented. It wasn't a "what" at all; she was a "who." She was three-and-a-half years old. She had been orally raped by her foster father; symptoms of gonorrhea had been found in her mouth.

Statistics at this level are not sterile, they are sobering. Imagine a chart that contained not only 715 marks representing sexually abused children from one county in one small state, but contained 135,750 marks from across the nation. Each of these marks is of great significance; each of these marks represents great suffering and loss.

## CHART #1
## CHILD ABUSE INVESTIGATIONS—1990
### Middlesex County, Massachusetts
### Total Population: 1,398,468

| SEXUAL ABUSE | SEXUAL ABUSE, CONTINUED | SEXUAL & PHYSICAL ABUSE |
|---|---|---|
| 1111111111 | 1111111111 | 1111111111 |
| 1111111111 | 1111111111 | 1111111111 |
| 1111111111 | 1111111111 | 1111111111 |
| 1111111111 | 1111111111 | |
| 1111111111 | 1111111111 | TOTAL: 30 |
| 1111111111 | 1111111111 | |
| 1111111111 | 1111111111 | |
| 1111111111 | 1111111111 | HOMICIDE & |
| 1111111111 | 1111111111 | PHYSICAL ABUSE |
| 1111111111*100 | 1111111111  *500 | |
| 1111111111 | 1111111111 | 1111111111 |
| 1111111111 | 1111111111 | 1111111111 |
| 1111111111 | 1111111111 | 1111111111 |
| 1111111111 | 1111111111 | 1111111111 |
| 1111111111 | 1111111111 | 11111 |
| 1111111111 | 1111111111 | |
| 1111111111 | 1111111111 | TOTAL: 45 |
| 1111111111 | 1111111111 | |
| 1111111111 | 1111111111 | |
| 1111111111 *200 | 1111111111  *600 | |
| 1111111111 | 1111111111 | OTHER |
| 1111111111 | 1111111111 | |
| 1111111111 | 1111111111 | 11111 |
| 1111111111 | 1111111111 | 11 |
| 1111111111 | 1111111111 | |
| 1111111111 | 1111111111 | TOTAL: 7 |
| 1111111111 | 1111111111 | |
| 1111111111 | 1111111111 | |
| 1111111111 | 11111 | |
| 1111111111 *300 | | |
| 1111111111 | TOTAL: 685 | |
| 1111111111 | | |
| 1111111111 | | |
| 1111111111 | | |
| 1111111111 | | |
| 1111111111 | | |
| 1111111111 | | |
| 1111111111 | | |
| 1111111111 | | |
| 1111111111 *400 | | |

## CHART #2
## CHILD SEXUAL ABUSE CHARGES—1990
Middlesex County, Massachusetts

| INDECENT ASSAULT: UNDER 14 | INDECENT ASSAULT: OVER 14 | RAPE OF A CHILD | ASSAULT WITH INTENT TO RAPE |
|---|---|---|---|
| 1111111111 | 1111111111 | 1111111111 | 111111111 |
| 1111111111 | 1111111111 | 1111111111 | |
| 1111111111 | 1111111111 | 1111111111 | TOTAL: 9 |
| 1111111111 | 1111111111 | 1111111111 | |
| 1111111111 | 111 | 1111111111 | |
| 1111111111 | | 1111111111 | UNSPECIFIED |
| 1111111111 | TOTAL: 43 | 1111111111 | SEXUAL |
| 1111111111 | | 1111111111 | ASSAULT |
| 1111111111 | | 1111111111 | |
| 1111111111 *100 | | 1111111111 *100 | 1111111111 |
| 1111111111 | | 1111111111 | 1111111111 |
| 1111111111 | | 1111111111 | 1111111111 |
| 1111111111 | | 1111111111 | 1111111111 |
| 1111111111 | | 1111111111 | 1111111111 |
| 1111111111 | | 1111111111 | 1111111111 |
| 1111111111 | | 1111111111 | 1111111111 |
| 1111111111 | | 1111111111 | 1111111111 |
| 1111111111 | | 1111111111 | 1111111111 |
| 1111111111 *200 | | 1111111111 | 111111 |
| | | 1111111111 *200 | |
| TOTAL: 200 | | 1111111111 | TOTAL: 96 |
| | | 1111111111 | |
| | | 1111111111 | |
| | | 1111111111 | EXPLOITATION |
| | | 1111111111 | |
| | | 1111111111 | 111111 |
| | | 1111111111 | |
| | | 1111111111 | TOTAL: 6 |
| | | 1111111111 *300 | |
| | | 1111111111 | |
| | | 1111111111 | |
| | | 1111111111 | INDECENT |
| | | 1111111111 | EXPOSURE |
| | | 1111111111 | |
| | | 1111111111 | 1 |
| | | | TOTAL: 1 |
| | | TOTAL: 360 | |

Middlesex County District Attorney, Thomas F. Reilly, comes even one step closer to the reality of child sexual abuse. And because of his proximity, he doesn't need statistics or studies or charts to be convinced of the severity of the problem. As county prosecutor, Reilly sees, first-hand, the painful effects and destructive after-effects of child sexual abuse. Knowing that the reported cases represent only the tip of the iceberg of actual cases, Reilly suspects that the sexual abuse of children has become an accepted part of our culture, even though it is morally and legally wrong. He believes that child sexual abuse has reached the status of a "moral emergency."[21] District Attorney Reilly is convinced that people in our society don't acknowledge or deal with a lot of social issues, especially if they don't think the issues affect them personally. But the long, documented, violent history of child sexual abuse has and does affect every human being.

Since the beginning of recorded history, there have been legal prohibitions against the use of children for sex by adults. And one has to wonder why, when the same laws that steadfastly exist today also existed so long ago, does the plague of child sexual abuse rage on? It seems, perhaps, that the success of a system or law can be attributed to the morals of the people working it or upholding it, rather than to any virtue in the system or law themselves.[22]

Professionals in the fields of social work, psychology and medicine believe that most abusers were, at one time, also victims. In his early work, psychiatrist Roland C. Summit referenced the "intergenerational chain of child abuse."[23] Using dramatic case studies, including Adolf Hitler, psychologist Alice Miller concluded:

> It is very difficult for people to believe the simple fact that every persecutor was once a victim. Yet it should be very obvious that someone who was allowed to feel free and strong from childhood does not have the need to humiliate another person.[24]

District Attorney Reilly's empirical experience with perpetrators of violent crimes, and abusers of drugs and alcohol, provides supporting evidence of repeated, future victimization by past victims. He indicated that the connection between childhood abuse and subsequent violence became especially evident and distressing during investigations into the lives of children who are charged with committing murder.[25] Even after the abuse has stopped, the pain lives on and is often the fuel for future abuse—of the self or others.

"There is a sad, self-preserving irony about a world that cannot see its own cruelty filled with victims who can't give voice to their pain."[26] And because of this desire for self-preservation by denial, we generally do not see or hear television news reports about 135,750 children being sexually abused in the United States; nor do we read in *The Boston Globe* about 715 children being sexually abused in the neighborhoods of Massachusetts. Because this pervasive, insidious destruction happens behind the closed doors of private homes and is usually shrouded by presumed caretaking and love, society has refused to acknowledge its existence, refused to acknowledge its effects.[27]

If 135,750 American children were being sexually assaulted and raped in Saudi Arabia, if 715 Massachusetts children were being sexually assaulted and raped at the Harvard Square subway station in Cambridge, surely our society would respond with righteous outrage. But because the sexual abuse of children usually occurs in private,

> we pretend nobody is involved, even though the veterans may outnumber the recruits. We still act as if victims are freaks and as if it is a virtue to be ignorant of sexual victimization.[28]

If progress is to be made toward stopping child sexual abuse, we can no longer remain ignorant. Today, thousands of "veteran" adult survivors who were sexually abused as children are no longer silent. They are telling the secrets in hopes of

> inspiring all good people to act, to intervene, to notice and report, to change laws, to listen to survivors with belief and sympathy and outrage, and above all to assume responsibility for protecting all our children.[29]

In order to overcome the cultural resistance to making the changes necessary to protect children from abuse, it is essential to keep child sexual abuse a topic of open discussion and to insist that people witness its painful consequences.[30]

The battlefield which represents the greatest threat of destruction to the American people is not in any desert of any Middle Eastern country, but in our own backyards. The lives of thousands of children, the future of America, are destroyed every day and every night, right before our closed eyes and our deaf ears.

We learned from Vietnam that one need not die in battle to become a casualty. "The human costs, pain and suffering do not end when combat ends. More Vietnam veterans were lost from suicide and slower forms of suicide such as alcoholism and drug abuse, than were lost in battle."[31] The human cost, pain, and suffering endured by survivors of child sexual abuse parallel those of combat veterans in definition and duration. The costs do not end when the abuse stops, but relentlessly haunt survivors throughout their lives.

The victims of child sexual abuse are faced with the challenging dilemma of finding a way to implore the attention of society. In his book, *Johnny Got His Gun*, Dalton Trumbo wrote about a World War I soldier who believed he had found a way to get society's attention regarding war. This soldier lost his arms, legs, sight, hearing, sense of smell, and his capacity to speak. After years in the hospital, he finally learned to communicate by tapping his head in morse code. He desired to go out into the world to let people see what war truly does.

> He would be doing good, too, in a roundabout way. He would be an educational exhibit. People wouldn't learn much about anatomy from him, but they would learn all there was to know about war. That would be a great thing, to concentrate war in one stump of a body and to show it to people so they could see the difference between a war that's in newspaper headlines . . . and a war that is fought out lonesomely in the mud somewhere, a war between a man and a high explosive shell.[32]

Some destructive results of war are made visible; but the majority of the devastation is hidden from our eyes, protecting us from the true horror so we will continue to wage war, so we can continue to sleep at night. The majority of the devastation of child sexual abuse is also kept hidden. Only the stories of successful survivors who appear to be doing "fine" reach the media. Television cameras rarely take our eyes into the locked wards of mental institutions, or the streets where teenage runaways and prostitutes earn a living, or the prisons where the abused are condemned for repeating the violence done to them, or into the lives of pornographic models, or the lives of drug addicts and alcoholics who spend every conscious moment trying to suppress the nightmare they call life, or into the broken hearts of the countless millions of child victims who believe they were to blame for the sexual abuse. In our daily lives, we usually do not have to see the horrifying acts or the devastating effects of child sexual abuse.

The only way to experience the true human cost of child sexual abuse is with our ears and our hearts. To begin the shift in the collective consciousness, we need to care. We need to hear.

We need to HEAR NOW, and begin to break the cycle of intergenerational child sexual abuse. We need to HEAR NOW, so future children will not have to suffer the same despair and destruction that has haunted—and molded—human history.

# CHAPTER THREE

# Myths and Realities: How It Should Be, How It Is

## Myth #1

The sexual abuse of children is an occasional deviant act.

## Reality

The sexual abuse of children is a devastating, common-place fact of everyday life.
> —Florence Rush, *The Best Kept Secret*

## Myths Perpetrate Denial

Myths are stories which serve to unfold part of the worldview or explain practices or beliefs. The myths surrounding the issue of child sexual abuse cause the issue to be seriously misunderstood. Consequently, these myths are perpetrators of denial. They serve to support the continuation of sexual violence toward children. (And any sexual interaction with children *IS* violence because of the criminal nature of the act, even when force is not used. One of the definitions of "violent" offered by *Webster's New Collegiate Dictionary* includes "the state of being excited to the point of *loss of control*." An adult who has any kind of sexual involvement with a child has definitely lost control.)

The most common myths aim to convince us that child sexual abuse is an "occasional deviant act," and that incest is "taboo."[1] Historical and cultural denial have created an unconscious acceptance of these myths. Therefore, it is believed by many that the sexual abuse of children in America is not really a problem. In order to begin the essential shift in collective awareness, the inaccurate, unconscious myths must be dismantled and replaced by conscious realities.

## Myth #2

Watch out for *strangers*.

## Reality

Statistics compiled in 1991 by the Office of the Middlesex County District Attorney in Massachusetts indicate that *only 2.7% of the perpetrators of child sexual abuse are strangers to the child victim*. 42% of the victims of child sexual abuse are molested in their own homes by biological relatives. That number increases to 60% when abusers from within step-families, foster families, and adoptive families are included.[2]

## Elizabeth

### "Too Young to Remember"

I was in my early 40s before I remembered. And when I finally did remember, it was like someone turned on a home movie that played on the screen of my brain. Memories that were so close to the surface. I knew I'd known the whole thing always, but at the same time was afraid to know.

When the film started rolling, I was in the coal cellar with my father and my grandmother. I could feel the cellar, smell the cellar. I could see the sun coming in through the window. I was only two when I came upon them in the cellar. They were sexually involved, and when I discovered them, they involved me. I heard my grandmother's voice. "Don't worry, Sarge, she's too young to remember." As the film continued rolling on the screen in my brain, I saw the orange-colored leaf in the fabric of my grandmother's dress. I've always hated orange.

My father left my family when I was three, but my grandmother continued to abuse me until I was seven. And maybe she was right: I was too young to consciously remember the sexual abuse at the time, but "hints" were always there.

And I never forgot that abuse was supposed to be a part of my life. I've been an overachiever forever. This has been great for those I've worked for, but "doing it all" has been very hard on me. I was a battered wife, and my daughter was raped by my second husband. My mother has always been abusive to me by denying all of my professional successes, by almost denying my existence.

When I see what incest has done to my life, I have no framework of reality. It has hurt me in so many ways, in every aspect of my life. Professionally and financially it has hurt me, and in every one of my relationships. Most importantly, though, it has negatively affected my relationship to myself.

A tragedy.[3] ❖

## Joe

### "My Best Friend"

I'm 16 years old now, and a junior in high school. When I was a kid, I was sexually abused by my best friend.

Bob moved into my neighborhood when I was eight. He bought the house on the corner and right away started fixing up the basement. The neighborhood guys would all hang around on Saturdays and watch him. Sometimes he'd even let us help. He built an awesome "Rec Room" with a pool table, pin-ball, a big screen TV for video games, and a bar with a Budweiser sign that lit up. He even had an old-fashioned juke-box with lots of old records. We used to give him a hard time about being an "oldie but a goodie," and that first Christmas, all the guys chipped in and bought him a cassette player and some updated music. In the Spring, we talked Bob into being a youth leader for our neighborhood club.

Bob was about 40 and divorced. He used to always say how much he missed his family, and that being around the guys made him feel better. My mom said she thought it was strange that Bob didn't seem to have a woman friend, because mom thought he was handsome and very nice. But Bob said he worked too much and didn't have time for women. I never did know what Bob worked too much doing, but he wore a suit, carried a black briefcase, and took the bus downtown every week day.

Sometimes the guys would go over to Bob's house on week nights, especially after the Jefferson Avenue Neighborhood Club meetings. But mostly we went over on Saturdays, and on Sundays, too, if we could. Being with Bob was always fun. We played games and goofed around and talked. Bob was great. He was someone I could really talk to. My dad worked downtown, too, and he was usually pretty tired when he came home. But Bob was never too tired for me. Bob was like a friend, and he was like a dad, too. He taught me to smoke like a friend, and helped me to figure things out like a dad. Bob had time for all the guys. He took us places, bought us presents, and gave us a space to just "hang out."

At first when we started spending time at Bob's house, he gave us candy and stuff, but then he started to encourage us to drink. In fact, on Saturdays he would make a special trip to the liquor store to buy whatever we wanted. We tried all different kinds of beer and wine and hard liquor. Bob said he was teaching us to drink in a safe and controlled environment so we wouldn't get in trouble out on the streets. I thought that was so cool of him, I wished my dad could be like Bob.

One Saturday morning, about 4 or 5 months after Bob moved into the neighborhood, I noticed a dirty magazine on the bar. I checked it out and then showed it to the other guys. When Bob saw what we were up to, he seemed a little nervous. He said some grown-up friends had been over the night before and the magazine had been left out by accident. He took it away from us. But about a month later, more magazines showed up. From then on, Bob started to get physical with us. He said he was teaching us about sex so we would be prepared, you know, for dating and stuff. Just like teaching us to drink for our own good, Bob said the sex was for our own good. It went on for years, and Bob made us promise never to tell anyone about our "private club," and especially never to tell about our "activities."

I liked all the attention Bob gave me. But the sex part felt so confusing—good and bad. I was almost 13 when I stopped going to Bob's. I don't remember why I stopped, but I just did. I was confused and really depressed because Bob and I couldn't be friends anymore. I really missed him. I missed all the fun we had. But I kept my promise. I didn't tell . . . for what seemed like a long, long, time I didn't tell. But then I did.[4] ❖

## Watch Out For . . .

In the late summer of 1990, I saw a flyer identifying a missing child posted at the Park Street subway station in downtown Boston. 13-year-old Melissa Benoit of Kingston, Massachusetts had been missing for several days. The flyer, which carried Melissa's photograph, noted when and where she was last seen and what she had been wearing: shorts and a T-shirt. The approaching Fall had brought a sudden cold snap to New England. I remember studying this flyer and considering Melissa Benoit's situation. Hoping Melissa had run away, I wished her a warm place and a coat to wear.

As it turned out, Melissa Benoit didn't need a coat. A few days later, her body was found buried in the basement of her neighbor's home. Melissa had been raped and murdered by her long-time neighbor, a well-respected, middle-aged man who was the head deacon of a local church.

A resident of Kingston, who knew both the victim and the perpetrator, poignantly juggled the myth. "You used to tell your children to watch out for strangers, but when you start telling them to watch out for people they know, well it's very confusing for small children. It's confusing for me."[5]

The stereotypes of child molesters as dirty old men, being psychotic, having a nervous breakdown and all of a sudden acting impulsively, or being retarded, don't hold up.[6] There is no "profile" description to use for warning children. "These sex offenders look like everybody else and there is really no way to physically distinguish such individuals from the rest of us."[7]

"[My father] was a 'pillar of the community' and a 'good provider.' Nobody would have believed that this man would do such a thing."[8]

Child molesters come from every economic class, cultural background, race and religion; the majority are

> likely to be very highly moral people in other aspects of their lives. They have a very strong, definite sense of what is right and wrong . . . and a distorted view of themselves and the effect they have on their victims. In fact, they don't see the child as the victim, but as benefitting from the relationship.[9]

I thought I was doing her a favor. I made myself feel that I was not doing anything wrong, that I was actually sexually educating her. We never did have complete intercourse. I thought . . . just touching and playing and fondling and all that, that wasn't harmful.[10]

As a parent, it is "standard procedure" to warn small children against taking candy from strangers and getting into cars with people they do not know. Attempting to dismantle this myth, that children are abused by strangers, has the potential to create chaos in our society. Imagine the uproar if, in the Sexual Abuse Prevention Programs in schools and churches, children were taught to watch out for their parents and relatives.[11] The idea would, of course, meet with resistance and total rejection. However, the undeniable facts remain: children are sexually abused by people they know and trust and love.

The violation of this innocent trust is an atrocious crime; yet it often goes unacknowledged, and usually goes unpunished. According to Boston therapist Linda T. Sanford, child molesters in the United States are rarely caught or punished. In order for a molester to actually be sentenced to prison, he or she has to make that particular goal a "mission" by being repetitive, violent, or abusing a number of children.[12]

Some researchers believe that such "widespread sexual abuse of children can only occur with at least the unconscious complicity of the [children's] parents."[13] Perhaps this is true in some cases of child sexual abuse, but we want to use extreme caution regarding this statement, and not mistakenly blame the victims of the crime and their families rather than the perpetrators. However, there are things parents unwittingly do which could place their children at risk. The simple act of teaching young children to "obey" relatives, baby-sitters and adult friends . . . could put children at risk. And the illegitimate and inappropriate use of the Judeo-Christian commandment "Honor your father and mother," often supports the manipulation of children into blind obedience of their parents, and creates a particular dilemma—not to mention a religious crisis—for children who are being sexually abused by their parents.

If the parent misuses this teaching to demand unquestioning obedience from a child, then the incest victim is

compelled to submit to sexual activity with
and to feel guilty if he/she questions such act

The child who discloses sexual abuse by a par....
plicitly challenges a traditional and cherished social
value, the right of a [parent] to do as he [she] pleases in
his [her] own home. And in effect, if not by intention,
society punishes the child who has the temerity to accuse
[the parent].[15]

In American culture, the family is an extremely private,
isolated social institution. Most other institutions in our society
are public and thereby benefit from a deliberate system of
checks and balances. According to ethicist James Gustafson, instability within the family can cause instability within the society; the family, although private and isolated, is interdependent
upon other social institutions, and vice versa.[16] Child sexual
abuse, therefore, not only harms individuals and disrupts
families but threatens to harm and disrupt all of society. "If incestuous abuse is indeed an inevitable result of family structure, then preventing sexual abuse will ultimately require a
radical transformation of the family [within society]."[17]

District Attorney Reilly provided a common and prag-
matic example regarding the interdependence of social institutions. He sadly experiences how the economics of our society
contribute to the continued sexual abuse of children. Often, the
primary family provider, usually a male, is the perpetrator; in
many instances, the child's mother stops the prosecution process by refusing to allow the child to testify. If the family provider is sentenced to jail, the mother will be saddled with the
responsibilities of parenting and supporting her children all
alone. Given the options, many women choose to sacrifice
their children for financial security.[18]

Perhaps the threat of potential disruptions in society is
one reason, the major reason, why the subject of sexual abuse
of children by family members is almost totally avoided. "One
of the clues to how important [this issue of child sexual abuse]
is, may be the effort devoted to keeping it out of sight."[19] "We
have overlooked or outrageously trivialized this subject, not because it is peripheral to major social interests, but because it is
so central that we have not yet dared to conceptualize its
scope."[20] Given that the epidemic of child sexual abuse is currently raging in the United States, it seems that both past and

current institutions of "family" have been unable to provide the necessary protection to children. Perhaps the solution involves the intervention of social institutions beyond the existing social service agencies. Perhaps it is time for the institutions of church and school to provide the necessary checks on the institution of family. Children must be protected from sexual abuse; adults must be held accountable for their actions. The efforts of the social service agencies charged with protecting children and the justice system, although admirable and relentless, are limited in their effectiveness by definition, economics and staffing.

"[The] visionary changes in the structure of the family, [and the family within society] will not be the work of one lifetime."[21] But we must begin. And we must begin now!

## Myth #3

Say NO. The abuse will stop.
You will be safe and protected.

## Reality

And Tamar took the cakes she had made, and brought them into the chamber to Amnon, her brother. But when she brought them near him to eat, he took hold of her, and said to her, "Come, lie with me, my sister." She answered him, "No my brother, do not force me; for such a thing is not done in Israel; do not do anything so vile . . ." But he would not listen to her; and being stronger than she, he forced her, and lay with her.

—NRSV 2 Samuel 13:10-14

## Hannah

### *"When I was ten."*

Dreaming, I think. Was I? I heard footsteps quietly moving up the stairs. He sat beside me on my bed. His presence woke me. Even in a half-sleep I knew I was frightened. And as I began to understand, I resisted him. I struggled. Awakened with terror, I fought wildly, pounding my fists at him, kicking. He held my wrists tightly and watched me struggle. Finally he spoke. He said, "You like it, you know you like it." I pleaded, "NO. NO. I hate it. I hate you. Please don't do this, Dad. Please, NO." Seeming amused, he allowed the struggle to continue. He grinned that familiar, sickening grin. Seeing it made my stomach turn over. Then he laughed. He mocked me as I struggled and cried. In a flash, his laughter became rage. "Stop that, stop that," he screamed in a whisper. His stinging slap startled me. I was instantly still and quiet. He laughed again. Part of me died and I became limp in surrender. I turned my face away, breathless, crying hot, silent tears. My eyes were open wide, staring blankly into the pain, humiliation and fear. My heart was pounding, pounding, pounding in my throat. Reaching toward the edges of the bed, he stretched my arms out. Vulnerable. I felt exposed, helpless. As he hovered over me on the bed, he forced his knees in between my legs. He knelt between my legs and pushed my knees apart with his own. My eyes pleaded with him. Please let me go, Dad. But he didn't see me. He seemed to be somewhere else. He just kept smiling. Staring blindly beyond me. Then he pulled my arms behind my head and held both of my wrists with one big hand. With his free hand he pulled up his faded paisley nightshirt and IT was there, bouncing. IT was smiling, too. He opened my body with his fingers. I cringed at his cold touch; tense, stiff, frozen. He closed his eyes. His face had an expression of far-away pleasure. He moaned softly. I felt IT begin to push against me. Fleshy, clammy, hard.

I remember no more except the quiet, endless tears. Left alone in the pain, I curled onto my side with my knees to my chin. Clutching that violated place between my legs with one hand, the fingers of my other hand in my mouth, stuffing down the sobs. Rocking, rocking until the sun began to peak through the shades on my windows.[22] ❖

## Who Should Say 'No'?

Throughout the past decade, an effort to educate children—the actual and potential victims—about sexual abuse has become a major movement in the United States. This effort is named "prevention" and its primary thrust involves teaching children—in schools, churches and clubs—about their bodily integrity and to "say no" if someone molests them. This movement has gained the support of professionals and survivors alike.

> Prevention of child sexual abuse should begin early in grade school. . . . In addition to basic information on sexual relations and assaults, children need to know that they have the right to their own bodily integrity.[23]

> Incest can only happen in secret. If parents, preferably both parents, sit down with a child at the age of 4 or 5 or whenever they tell her about not getting into cars with strangers and so forth—and at the same time tell the child that no one has a right to touch her in certain ways, not even if it's someone she knows and loves—that child is being given a power she needs.[24]

> Nobody, not even your parents, has the right to do anything to your mind or body that makes you feel bad or uncomfortable. And you are right to want to put an end to it. It is your body and you can say "no" without feeling guilty.[25]

Any message that communicates their worth and dignity and bodily integrity to children is a valuable one. It is not, however, a particularly effective way to stop child sexual abuse because there remains THE QUESTION OF POWER. "In relations with adults, there is no way that a child can be in control or exercise free choice."[26] Often adults don't comprehend this concept because "the intrinsic helplessness of a child clashes with the cherished adult sense of free will";[27] but in reality, "no child has equal power to say no to a parental figure or to anticipate the consequences of sexual involvement with an adult caretaker."[28]

*Breaking Silence,* a videotape which presents the disclosures and personal accounts of several adult survivors of child sexual abuse, includes a segment on a pre-school class learning to "say no" when someone touches them "in a way they don't like." The message is powerful and important, but for the kids, it was clearly a game. The children took turns jumping up from their chairs, and with their fingers in their mouths—in between their squeals and giggles—they would forcelessly say, or mumble, or whisper, a barely audible "no."[29]

This visual experience depicted for me, beyond any myth or doubt, the ineffectiveness of any child's protest. In 1991, *With the Best of Intentions: The Child Sexual Abuse Prevention Movement*, by Jill Duerr Berrick and Neil Gilbert of the University of California at Berkeley, was published. This book supported the doubts I experienced while watching *Breaking Silence*. Berrick and Gilbert urge a "cautionary look at the child sexual abuse prevention movement,"[30] and literally challenge the basis of these programs. They call into question the effectiveness of the ideology of empowerment, which grew out of the women's movement, when it is applied to young children.[31] Even if children do learn to say "no" at school or at church, even if they do say "no" when people touch them, it is no more than wishful denial to believe that children's protests will stop child molesters. "If an adult insists upon a sexual relationship with a dependent child, the child *will* comply."[32]

Since many perpetrators of child sexual abuse were also abused as children, it can be assumed that they, too, suffer the effects of those childhood experiences. As adult survivors, abusers commonly suppress their memories and their pain with drugs, alcohol, work, violence and sexual perversions.[33] Most often, the people who sexually abuse children are addicted to what they do. They enjoy the emotional and physical results of their sexual "fix," and will not stop of their own accord. Therefore, efforts to stop child molesters must be severe enough and forceful enough to substantially outweigh the pleasurable sexual experiences.[34] In general, child molesters are not especially polite or responsive to the needs of others.[35] And certainly, molesters caught in the power of their addiction will not comply with the fearful, feeble requests of a child. In reality, the child victims of sexual abuse are saying "no" or "stop" or "don't" or "I don't want to," usually to no avail. The adult survivors also said "no"—30, 40, 500, 4000 years ago, again to no avail.[36]

Supporting, developing, and implementing prevention programs directed at a child population is important; however, if this is the *only* effort made to protect children from sexual abuse, the children will surely remain at risk. Children saying "no" as an effective method of preventing child sexual abuse is

a myth because "the final choice in the matter of sexual relations between adults and children rests with the adult."[37]

If the goal is to prevent children from being sexually
abused, perhaps it is *adults* who need educating; perhaps it is
adults who need to learn about the inherent worth and dignity
and the bodily integrity of children; perhaps it is adults who
need to learn to say "no" to their own destructive tendencies
and actions.

## Myth #4

If children *TELL* someone that they are being sexually
abused, they will be believed, they will be helped, and
the abuse will stop.

## Reality

See, I never told because I just knew my parents . . . I
knew there was no way . . . there just was no way I was
going to be believed if I went to them.
—Survivor of Child Sexual Abuse, *Kiss Daddy Goodnight*

## Chloe

### "Why Didn't You Tell Me?"

My Mom asked me that—twice—after I told her I had
been molested by my Dad. The first time she asked, she was
sympathetic, supportive and kind. I was not prepared for this
type of loving reaction. Was this really MY Mom?

I told her over the phone because we live quite a distance
apart. She knew something was wrong, but for six months I
had been keeping the things that were happening in my life
very much to myself. But now, after a 12-week incest support
group, I knew it was time to tell her the truth of what I had
remembered. And so I called her.

And I just told her. My heart pounding practically out of
my chest. "Dad molested me." Her reply definitely shocked
me. "I thought that's what it might be. Oh honey, I'm so
sorry. This explains so much. But why didn't you tell me?" I

answered her question with a question. "If I had told you, what would you have done?" She answered without leaving even a second for thought. "Well, I would have thrown him out and divorced him."

My heart was warmed by Mom's reaction to my first disclosure of incest, and although I wanted to bask in her support, I somehow didn't fully trust her words. Her reaction was pretty out of character. And besides, it was easy for her to say she would have divorced Dad. It was a moot point, after all. He'd been dead for 17 years.

Slowly the demon of denial began to creep back into Mom's life. She struggled with insomnia, a problem she had never before experienced. During those dark, sleepless hours she began to doubt and disbelieve the horrible truth. She had married and lived with a child molester. Her support eventually faded into the complete denial of my truth.

Three months later, Mom came to visit me. I wanted her to go with me to see my therapist. I was surprised when she agreed to go. It was there that she asked me for the second time, "Why didn't you tell me?" But her tone had changed from one of support into an accusation, an attempt to discredit me. Before I could answer, she continued. "You and I were pals when you were little. You told me everything. You would've told me this. Besides you were such a tattletale. You told on everyone and it used to just burn me up."

I floundered in silent tears for several minutes before I could respond. I reminded Mom of my last visit to her home, my childhood home, which had occurred at Christmastime three years earlier.

Mom had a boyfriend. Finally! Her first since Dad had died. I was so happy for them. When I arrived at the airport, Mom and Martin were there together, waiting to meet me. Mom hugged me, and then introduced me to Martin. He hugged me, too. The next night, Martin and I were alone in the living room while Mom was in the kitchen preparing dinner. We were standing, facing each other. I don't know why. Martin moved toward me, with his arms open as if to hug me. I remember that it seemed to be a strange or inappropriate gesture, but I thought, "He's Mom's friend, it's okay." As he got closer to me, I realized that he intended to kiss me on the cheek! He moved closer still, and without warning, he turned his head and kissed me on the mouth, shoving his 71-year-old tongue between my lips and into my mouth. Oh, gross! I was totally shocked and disgusted, but I didn't say even a word about it to Martin. And I still wonder why I didn't confront him right then, but maybe I didn't want to be rude to my mother's friend, or maybe I had been trained not to challenge men, not to make waves. But I did march right into the kitchen to tell Mom. "Mom, Martin just gave me a kiss and stuck his tongue into my mouth." Without even looking up from the food she was preparing, she dismissed me casually by saying, "Oh yes, I know. He does that to me sometimes, too, and I don't like it either."

Maybe I did tell you about Dad. Maybe you didn't hear me then. Maybe you responded in the same way that you did that night when Martin kissed me. Maybe I tried to tell you again. Maybe I stopped telling you, stopped trying.

Angry, Mom lashed out at me. "Why are you still talking about Martin? Besides, I asked him and he said he didn't do that." An adult now, and safe in the office of my therapist, I stood up to her. "Mom, I was 32 years old. I was completely sober. I came to you immediately and told you what Martin had done."

She couldn't deny it anymore. My clarity, consistency and certainty about the event simply could not be challenged. Since she couldn't deny Martin's kiss, her next defense was to diminish it. "Well, what does it mean anyway? He just darts his tongue in and out so quickly. Then it's over. So what's the big deal?"

Your response makes me sick, Mom. But I think it does answer the question that you asked me. I didn't tell you because I knew that you wouldn't or couldn't hear me. I knew that you weren't on my side. Not then, not now.[38] ❖

## Listening and Hearing Are Necessary

Child victims of sexual abuse face secondary trauma in the crisis of discovery. Their attempts to reconcile their private experience with the realities of the outer world are assaulted by the disbelief, blame and rejection they experience from adults. [The child is stigmatized] with charges of lying, manipulating or imagining.[39]

Encouraging children who are being sexually abused to TELL is in direct opposition to the threatening demands for secrecy the children receive from the perpetrators. Most children are frightened by their abusers "into life-long silence."[40]  "To tell would be to risk the wrath of the molester and possibly to destroy the family.  To remain in silence is to risk further *abuse . . . Such heavy burdens for such small shoulders!*"[41]

In order for the victims of child sexual abuse to begin the healing process, they must disclose the abuse.  Thus, encouraging them to "TELL" is a healthy message.  However, the word "disclose," which is considered the clinical and legal description of revealing an incident of sexual abuse, means much more than merely "tell."  Disclose means to open up, to expose to view, or to make known something previously held as secret.  This literal definition of the word helps us to understand that when victims and survivors disclose, they are entrusting more to us than mere words, or the facts of an incident.  They open, expose and reveal themselves, and are thus extremely vulnerable to whomever they tell.

Therefore, teaching children to TELL is not the first step in the process of stopping the current abuse, protecting the children from repeated abuse, and holding the offender accountable.  I offer THREE steps which are necessary to take before placing *the burden of telling* on the child victims.

**STEP ONE:** If, in Sexual Abuse Prevention Programs, children are being educated and encouraged to TELL, then increased awareness and sensitivity to the issue *by the adult population* is essential.  When courageous child victims of sexual abuse do tell someone, that someone needs to be prepared to hear and to believe the child.

In her book, *The Best Kept Secret,* social worker Florence Rush concluded that incest is not taboo at all; but that *talking* about incest is![42]  But I'm not convinced about this.  While doing research into the issue, I discovered 5000 years of consecutive, historical documentation of child sexual abuse, ranging from Sumerian clay tablets, the Code of Hammurabi, and The Hebrew Bible, to the writings of 20th-century female authors.  Since so much documented evidence of child sexual abuse exists, I must conclude that during these past 5000 years the victims were talking . . . and writing . . . and drawing.  And so I wonder . . . Is *hearing* the small voices of the children as they describe their trauma and everlasting pain what is really taboo?

Having their disclosure heard can literally be a lifesaving experience for both child victims and adult survivors of child sexual abuse.

> My mother gave me the gift of anger, the strength and healing power of fury and direct action. My mother believed me, she vindicated me, she protected me. I learned I could protect myself. I was not prey. I felt safe.[43]

> Disclosure of sexual abuse and how the disclosure is handled by adults significant in the victim's life is also an important aspect that may in part determine the adjustment of the victim and those who share [his or] her life.[44]

Although disclosure can be helpful and healing, often victims resist their desire and their need to tell someone because they are trapped into silence "by a suspicion that [they] had something to do with all of it."[45] In order for telling to be truly helpful, victims and survivors need to feel confident that they will be *heard* and *believed* and *vindicated*. They must be heard. They must be believed. They must be vindicated.

**STEP TWO:** Although laws which protect children from sexual abuse are currently in place, the legal process needs to be changed to accommodate the needs and rights of children.

Over the years, the laws have been evaluated and revised and some of the responsibility for telling has shifted from the child victims onto the adults working with them. Chapter 119, the Massachusetts Child Abuse Reporting Law, was revised in 1973 to include "mandated reporting." This revision required certain individuals who work with children [i.e., teachers, social workers, therapists, physicians] to report abuse or suspected abuse of children to the Department of Social Services (DSS). Known failure to report requires prosecution. In 1983 the law was again revised by Chapter 288, and DSS was required to report child abuse to the District Attorney. Following the implementation of Chapter 288, the number of child sexual abuse cases investigated by the Middlesex County District Attorney rose dramatically from 207 in 1984 to 715 in 1990.[46]

Although District Attorney Reilly believes the threat of prosecution can be an effective intervention in deterring this

crime, he believes the only way to accomplish widespread re-
duction of child sexual abuse is a shift in attitude regarding the
rights and needs of children. Reilly hopes the justice system
can be forceful enough in the prosecution of child sexual abuse
offenses to create an awareness of right and wrong in regard to
this crime, which apparently does not currently exist.[47]

However, due to the basic assumptions and inherent limitations governing the justice system, the prosecution of child
sexual abuse cases cannot be relied upon as the sole source of
accountability for this crime and sin. That a defendant is innocent until proven guilty beyond a reasonable doubt is the "cor-
nerstone of the American criminal justice system."[48] But when
the only witness to the crime is a two-year-old victim with a
venereal disease, rarely can the identity of the perpetrator be
proved beyond a reasonable doubt. If the child is older and
can demonstrate his or her competency as a witness, court testi-
mony is possible; but often the victim refuses to testify out of
fear, shame, or doubt; often the victim's family is not supportive and will not allow the child to be a witness; often the victim
is psychologically unstable and testifying would not be in his
or her best interest.[49]

The court process can be yet another trauma for the child
victim. The defendant possesses the right of confrontation, so
the child must appear in the courtroom, face the abuser, disclose the humiliating facts of the sexual abuse to a judge and a
jury of strangers, and be cross-examined by the defense attorney. This process is distressing, at best, even for adults, and
rarely are accommodations made to ease the distress of child
witnesses.

The courtroom is a scary, foreign place—especially for
children—and the accommodations in the system necessary for
them to testify successfully are rarely made. In his trial in Athens 2500 years ago, even Socrates requested accommodations:

> The truth is this: I am more than seventy, and this is the
> first time that I have ever come before a law court; thus
> your manner of speech here is quite strange to me. If I
> had really been a stranger, you would have forgiven me
> for speaking in the language and manner of my native
> country. And so now I ask you to grant me what I think I
> have a right to claim.[50]

Although the need for accommodations in the courtroom is obviously not a new or unique idea, rarely are children's needs taken into consideration in the adult legal environment. Just as individuals who speak foreign languages or are limited by handicaps are accommodated in court, child victims have a *right* to accommodations. They have a right to trust that everything possible has been done to help them avoid re-traumatization while seeking protection and justice. But even with accommodations, the truth is children will be distressed and frightened in court. This distress is often the end result of telling.

**STEP THREE:** Teaching and actively encouraging children to TELL should become the primary prevention focus only after the adults in our society—including judges and juries, priests, rabbis and ministers, teachers and doctors—are informed and knowledgeable about the issue of child sexual abuse, prepared to provide support and comfort, and truly available to listen and hear.

## Myth #5

They're just [children], *they'll be fine.*[51]

## Reality

Have you run across the people who say, "Why can't it be all right?" Oh, God. Tell them to ask somebody who's been through it.
—Survivor of Child Sexual Abuse, *Kiss Daddy Goodnight*

## Catherine

### "Fix It"

Pressure point. I can't hide this. Get help. Fix it, fix it, fix it, fix it, fix it, fix it, pleeeeease! Please fix it. I can't hide this! Please fix it! Make it all okay! Please fix it, fix it, fix it, fix it, fix it, fix it!

While wheeling me into the operating room, the nurse said to the surgeon that I had a self-inflicted five-inch gash on my upper left arm. I had to laugh, but I kept my laughter to myself because they wouldn't understand what was so funny.

It was funny because it was true. I had created a gash in my own flesh. And I mean "gash" in its most unpleasant usage.

I won't go into the gory details; you've heard stories like mine before. But I had been in therapy, for years, and had "come to terms" with what had happened. But there were no terms to come to. It wasn't my fault. I didn't have control. I was a child. He was my father. Et cetera.

Nearly every day, or every other day, some memory will rise up to the surface. Worse are the days when the memories linger just beneath the surface. You're not sure why you're depressed or angry, but you are sure that you are.

It was one of those days when the memories bobbed just beneath the surface. I had gotten a nasty phone call from a collection agency earlier in the day. I had had an argument with my mother on the telephone. I had not been able to complete my readings for class the next day.

I was making a picture frame for a family photograph. I was using a razor blade. My boyfriend called. We had an argument. I hung up on him. I cut myself.

It's really that simple. But it isn't.

I hadn't even been thinking about it. But it was there. It's always there. And now it was out in the open. I couldn't ignore it anymore, just as I couldn't ignore the gash in my arm. I needed to fix it. I needed to have someone else fix it. I needed help fast.

There should have been blood. There was lots of tissue spilling out of the gash, but no blood. There should have been blood.

How could there have been blood? I had been bled a long time ago.[52] ❖

## Faith

### *"Shameful Secrets"*

When I was a child, I was sexually assaulted by three different persons prior to the age of nine. Twice by males and once by a female. Each of these individuals were persons whom I turned to out of a deep sense of fear and pain resulting from mental and physical abuse I had been receiving at the hands of foster parents I had been placed with.

Both of the males involved in this sexual abuse were ordained representatives of the church, who had through their positions developed a very close relationship with me as substitute fathers. The female, who knew of the kind of physical and mental abuse I was receiving from my foster parents (she lived in the upstairs apartment which she rented from my foster parents), provided a very comfortable haven for me away from my foster parents. Actually I never thought of what she did to me as sexual abuse until several years ago.

When I had just turned nine years of age, I deliberately pushed my foster mother, who was close to 300 pounds, down the stairs of a major department store and stabbed my foster father in the chest with a butcher knife. Both of them lived, even though I prayed as hard as I could ever remember to Jesus Christ that they both should die. I have never told anyone the reasons for that action but I think the significance of that event is important to this presentation.

When I had turned eight years of age, I got very attached to one of my teachers who was also a minister in the church I attended. He was great at sports and taught science, one of the subjects I was really good at and loved. I was at the time a very mean-acting kid who was always into fights in school with the other kids. He also counselled the kids who were in trouble. He and I worked out this deal that I wouldn't fight in school during the week, but on Fridays after school I could put on the boxing gloves and duke it out in the gym privately. Well, he began to call me to help him in class and after school with various things that he paid me to do. He would get me passes to movies that I loved and would take me on trips to Coney Island and the Bronx Zoo . . . At various times he would ask permission of my foster parents for me to help him out on weekends so I would stay over at his place. At these times, we would bathe together and sleep in one bed. He was a very touchy kind of person who hugged a lot in private. At the time, I felt really strange about where and how he was touching me, but compared to the other comforts I was feeling, I sort of accepted it as part of the relationship. Just when I turned nine, he got permission for me to attend camp in Bear Mountain for two weeks with a group he was sponsoring through the church. I was sort of his chief honcho at the time and primarily stayed in the cabin with him rather than with the other kids. During that two-week period, I was sodomized nightly and forced to commit oral sex a number of times . . . The physical pain I was able to suppress in a way, for I thought of myself as a very tough kid hardened by the physical abuse I had been receiving for most of my life up until that time. It was the utter shame and the sense of violation I couldn't shake. It was clear to me when I left that camp that I could never for the rest of my life trust anyone. I could never talk to anyone about what happened, for the only person I could've talked to about such a thing was the very person who had done it to me.

For almost a month after that, I literally terrorized those who were around me. I remember almost smothering to death the child of my foster parents. I spent my days and nights thinking up ways to kill my foster parents, everything from burning down the house to putting rat poison in the food. Instead of going to church I would sneak off every Sunday, catch the subway and go to the movies. I dreaded the end of summer because I knew I would have to go back to church or school and run into this minister/teacher. The closer I got to this time the meaner I became and so just before I was to return to school I committed the act of pushing my foster mother down the stairs and plunging a knife in the chest of my foster father.

As one who was sexually abused let me state that writing this piece has not been very easy for me. And it will not be easy for those many amongst us to reveal their abuse, whether the very young or the very old. I don't know what life will hold for me, but I do know that there is real potential for me to function a little healthier because of my exposure of this most most shameful secret.

I sincerely hope it can encourage somone out there to do the same.[53] ❖

## Re-defining "Fine"

Unaware of or inattentive to the voices of the survivors, sociologist James Ramey published a "pro-incest manifesto" in a newsletter distributed by SIECUS, a respected national sex-education organization. Commenting on Ramey's manifesto, Judith Herman, author of *Father-Daughter Incest*, writes,

> Ramey equates the prohibition on incest with other sexual taboos that have not withstood scientific scrutiny. "We are roughly in the same position today regarding incest as we were a hundred years ago with respect to our fear of masturbation." On the question of harm, he argues, people are simply afraid to face the possibility that many, perhaps most, participants in incest suffer no dire consequences.[54]

Other organizations and "reasonable people"[55] agree with James Ramey, and believe that

> most sexual abuse is nonviolent, nonpenetrating and harmless. If there is harm, it results more from societal horror and criminalization than from the sexual experience itself.[66]

Are these people and organizations listening to the victims and survivors?

Even supportive family members and well-intentioned friends can inadvertently minimize the reality of child sexual abuse by urging victims to "put it in the past" and "get on with life." Although these "helpful" suggestions actually support the continuation of denial and trivialization of the effects of child sexual abuse, why loved ones would want the experience to be "past" is understandable. The relentless pain of victims and survivors is difficult to tolerate.

In spite of the urge to believe the myths and dismiss the realities so the horrible truth won't have to be faced, it must be remembered that the final judgement on the question of harm belongs solely to the child victims and the adult survivors who have endured the traumatic experience of child sexual abuse.

Although not all victims of child sexual abuse will suffer for life as a result of the experience, most are wounded and scarred in some way. The wounds often vary with the type and length of abuse, the age the abuse began and ended, the relationship of the child to the perpetrator, and the outcome following disclosure. Some victims display symptoms of mild neurosis; some victims present symptoms of multiple-personality disorder or schizophrenia. Some victims endure a lifetime of endless depression; some victims can't endure it and commit suicide.[57]

Over the past decade there has been an influx of professional support reaching out to victims and survivors of child sexual abuse, as well as the publication of numerous self-help books. These self-help books face a difficult challenge: giving victims and survivors hope for future healing without diminishing the effects of the abuse in the minds of the general public, the professionals working with the issue, or the victims and survivors themselves.

From a hopeful vantage point, professionals and authors alike profess that survivors of child sexual abuse can live full and fulfilling lives. They also agree that such fulfillment takes "work," but rarely is this "work" defined or described in any detail.

This hope for healing can lead to another difficult challenge. Survivors do need to hear that things are going to get better because if they don't hear it, if they don't believe it, it is feared that many, many more will kill themselves than already do. But while some survivors receive hope, others may become discouraged if they are not yet better, not yet "fine." Somewhere in the midst of the mysterious and excruciating "work," these struggling survivors feel lost and forgotten. They may begin to believe they have failed in the recovery process. In some ways, therefore, this broad range of hopeful literature does a disservice to the victims and survivors because it can feed denial. The general public reads that the victims of child sexual abuse can be fine and fulfilled, and they conclude: "It's not such a big problem after all. They were kids; there are books they can read; there is 'work' they can do; they'll be fine." The MYTH re-emerges, strengthened now by unintentional professional collusion.

Please, do not be fooled or cajoled by modern denial. Once a child has been sexually abused, *the damage*—whether reparable or not—*has been done.* And *it can never be assumed,* or even expected, that people who lived through and live with the trauma of child sexual abuse will automatically or easily be FINE.

## A Prayer for Survival

*Survivors: Please Hear Us, O People of God. We speak from our own experiences in a representative voice for all past, present and future victims of child sexual abuse.*

*Barbara:*

>I lived in constant fear most of my life.
>I just didn't know which way to turn, where to hide, what to do . . . every day of my life, I just wanted to die.[58]

*All: Hear Us, O People of God. Many of us experience overwhelming anxiety, confusion and despair.*

*Shane:*

>When I attempted suicide four years ago, I wanted my life to end. I was an abused child and later became an abuser; and I think that's more devastating than being abused. I got so fed up with the guilt and the pain and the abuse and abusing myself, that after dark I went downstairs to the basement and lit the garbage on fire and went back upstairs and went to bed. I prayed to God that night that I wouldn't wake up.[59]

*All: Hear Us, O People of God. Many of us abuse others.*

*Chris:*

>For most of my life I wandered aimlessly about, moving from place to place, job to job, relationship to relationship, addiction to addiction, trying desperately to suppress the pain that was destroying me from within like a cancer.[60]

*All: Hear Us, O People of God. Many of us are addicted to drugs and alcohol. We try to run away from the pain, but cannot; it is part of us.*

*Gayle:*   i'm a weak little girl
i don't know what's best for me
i depend on others to decide
i lean on others for strength
will i ever transcend this hostage existence?[61]

*Steve:*

The psychologically crippling effect on me was the hindering of my ability to perceive myself as a man, dealing with other men as a grown-up in the world. Somehow the experience of sexual abuse had told me that I was not an adult; that I was meant to be a boy. Carrying the overlay of the absence of my worth as an adult male was a burden to me, whether externally visible or not.[62]

*All: Hear Us, O People of God. Because of our low self-esteem, many of us will struggle to become independent adults.*

*Richard:*

I hope that any victim who is so arrogant and thinks that they can control things, as I did for so many years, would think differently and would not assume that they can go on indefinitely, because they may fail as I failed. And I hope that any adult who even, for a moment, might contemplate the idea of engaging with a child sexually, would realize that it's not only a crime and a sin, but they're planting a bomb, and that bomb is ticking, and it will go off. It might go off 24 hours later, or 24 years later, but it will go off.[63]

*All: Hear Us, O People of God. Please, before we explode.*

*Charlotte:*

Painstakingly, painfully, year after year, I've had to reach down through the layers of me to try to get at the truth, dredge it up and live trying to change it. Always in the back of my mind lives the knowledge that if I fail, I can open the door marked EXIT and walk through it via pills or razor blades or a gas oven or a slow walk into deep water.[64]

*All: Hear Us, O People of God.   Many of us contemplate, attempt or succeed at suicide.*

*Ann:*

At first, when I told her my father had sexually abused me, my mom believed me. But then she couldn't. She preferred to believe I was crazy. But when she finally came to see me, it was distressingly clear to her that I wasn't crazy. Since she still couldn't believe me about the abuse, she concluded that I hated her and made it up to hurt her. I can't even imagine what kind of terrible monster she must think I am to create such a nightmare for myself and my family. My father's been dead for almost 20 years, and now I realize I don't have a mother anymore either.[65]

*All: Hear Us, O People of God.   Sexual abuse destroys families.   Many of us have lost our families and feel that we have no one.*

*Karen:*

I have no self-esteem, none. I hate everybody.
I have no sexuality. I have no value. I have no friends, and I don't want any. I'm not a nice woman anymore. I spent all those years yessing people to death and being nice to everybody . . . And I'm bitter . . . That's a terrible way to be, to be so terribly abused that you hate everybody.[66]

*All: Hear Us, O People of God. Many of our souls have perished.*

*Kathy:*

> I can't get along with other people. I don't trust anyone . . . or I trust them too much. I have a regular pattern of destroying relationships.[67]

*All: Hear Us, O People of God. We have difficulty trusting and developing intimacy in relationships.*

*Beth:*    Why do I hurt so deeply
              it seems forever, this pain
    Why do I ache so
              with such intense sadness
              with so much confusion
              and so many tears
  So, so much loneliness?[68]

*All: Hear Us, O People of God. We are painfully isolated and alone.*

*Karen:*

> Many years later, I told my friend and lover about the [incest]. It was like a ghost returning as the familiar grin came to his face and he said, "You must have been a sexy little girl."[69]

*All: Hear Us, O People of God. Often we are blamed for the abuse. Help us to forgive ourselves.*

*Annamarie:*

> You want to destroy something, to go and do something to the cause of the problem. You want to lash out. Your senses have left. You feel numb, but you want someone to

die. You end up attacking yourself. Only you deserve the pain. to feel your own ANGER. . . .[70]

*All: Hear Us, O People of God. Many of us abuse ourselves. Help us learn to love ourselves.*

*Lucy:*

What do you do when you need someone to take care of you, and there is no one?[71]

*All: People of God, Hear Us Please. Our scars cannot be seen.*

# CHAPTER FOUR

# *A Sorrowful Road: A History of Child Sexual Abuse*

Who would not shudder if he were given the choice of
eternal death or life again as a child? Who would not
choose to die?

—St. Augustine, *City of God*

## Stephen (1)

### *"The Place Where It Happened"*

Not just "a lake"; Parks Pond is a real place, 18 miles east
of Bangor on Route 9.

You can see the cliff from the highway. Not just "a cliff";
on this one I focused my teenage need to end all pain. The lake
would sparkle as I launched myself from the top, scared free of
the earth and let go of even that sensation . . .

Highway 9 touches the north end of the pond. The stream
enters at the southern tip, not accessible by road or trail. Not
just "a stream"; this remains the hidden, lovely setting of
hemlocks and large glacial erratics my uncle and I explored
when I was 10. I am still powerfully drawn to such woods,
such discovery.

The boulder sets, car-sized, on a little rise 100 feet from
the shore. Not just "a boulder"; I was crushed down onto the
hood of this particular rock when my uncle raped me. Both of
us could see the lake through the trees; he to watch for
anyone's approach; myself, as the light beyond the pressing
shadow that suffocated me.

It happened, at this place. I could take you there to see
and touch the lake, the cliff, the stream, the rock.

And in my adolescent fantasies, escape meant disappearing underwater.[1] ❖

## Stephen (2)

### *"But Why?"*

Age 10: For months after that lake vacation I lived in terror of the hairbrush. There is something about me that makes my mother feel she has to use this weapon on me.
WHAT IS WRONG WITH ME?

Age 12: I am so alienated from my peers that, seeing me a block away, a group of classmates point and scream names at me.
WHY DO GIRLS HATE ME?

Age 15: My sexual fantasies are of being tied up with girls, of escaping by diving into Parks Pond with the girl I love and never needing to surface.
WHY?

Age 16: I write a painful fantasy about a boy trembling as he walks under the malevolent glare of houses. In the woods he takes off his clothes, runs heedlessly through the slashing brush, and plunges bloody and sweaty into a stream.
WHY DO I FRANTICALLY SCRIBBLE SUCH THINGS?

Age 16: I am suicidal, often fantasizing a painless fall from the high cliff over Parks Pond.
BUT WHY?

Age 21: The weekend of a formal event, many fraternity brothers have girlfriends staying over. I walk 10 miles to the George Washington Bridge, sit long on the Palisade cliffs looking down, walk the lonely miles back.
BUT WHY?

Age 22: I am afraid to be in the same room with any woman my age. A friend's wife learns to tolerate my mute presence, and I become utterly emotionally dependent on her.
BUT WHY?

Age 24: My first sexual relationship ends. I am hysterical, overwhelmed by a terrifying pain rising from within.
WHY? WHY?

Age 29: I become a father, and suddenly I cannot tolerate my sexuality. For years I rationalize about Gandhi-like celibacy, about abstention as needed in an overpopulated world.
BUT REALLY, WHY?

Age 34: I KNOW WHY. And I understand also why I forgot—how else could a 10-year-old cope with being raped.
For 24 years my own maleness seemed ugly to me, as had my uncle's at Park's Pond; I viscerally needed the love and feared the disapproval of women, as I had my mother's.
How old will I be by the time I heal the manifold re-openings of that wound?[2] ❖

## Pat

### *"Friday Comes"*

It's Saturday
> My body aches and my mind is foggy.
> I need to get out of bed and
> Face the week —
>> *But Friday comes*

It's Sunday
> What did I do wrong? I guess I
> deserved it. I'll try harder to
> do things right —
>> *But Friday comes*

It's Monday
> Do the kids at school know what happens?
> If only I could lift

> my head higher —
>> *But Friday comes*

It's Tuesday
> My mind is clearing and the bruises are healing.
> I guess I had
> that dream again —
>> *But Friday comes*

It's Wednesday
> I block out thoughts so they
> will go away. Why do I make
> up such things? —
>> *But Friday comes*

It's Thursday
> Why do I have this awful
> feeling of dread? Why do I feel
> so lost and alone? —
>> *But Friday comes*

It's Friday
> I've done everything right all
> week. This time it will be different.
> It won't happen again —
>> *But he comes*[3] ❖

## A 5000-Year-Long Nightmare

Child sexual abuse is a *REAL* problem, not just "really a problem." The accounts of sexual abuse, the statistics, and the psychological assessments are about real people—real feelings, real struggles, real anguish. Please do not forget, for even one second, while reading this interesting history of child sexual abuse that the journey through life, for each and every one of the billions of victims, could have been, could be, devastating.

*Victims of victims of victims of victims of victims* ... "Intergenerational chain of child abuse," the phrase used by Dr. Roland Summit, creates a visual image of the words "victims of victims" typed into infinity. Although the first link in this chain of child sexual abuse is undoubtedly unknown, we do know the chain is very long and very old. Five-thousand-year-old Sumerian clay tablets included accounts of, protests against, and laws governing the use of children for sex by adults.[4] The four-thousand-year-old Code of Hammurabi included punishments—chiseled in stone—for men who had intercourse with girls.[5] One has to wonder who the first victims were, and why.

In 1976 Susan Brownmiller, author of *Against Our Will*, named patriarchy as the root of the cause and the continuation of child sexual abuse. She re-named father-daughter incest "father rape," and offered an explanation for its relentless practice throughout antiquity, throughout history, into our lifetimes.

> . . . father rape has hardly been the universal or uncompromising taboo that psychologists and anthropologists would have us believe; or rather, the taboo against father rape is superseded by a stronger, possibly older taboo— there shall be no outside interference in the absolute dictatorship of father rule.[6]

I agree that the *system* of patriarchy contributes to the sexual abuse of children. However, this abuse is not necessarily caused by patriarchy. It is caused by more powerful people misusing their power over less powerful people. This abuse is caused by and continues because of . . . *people.*

I do not agree that the patriarch, the man, the father is the sole abuser of children. In the hierarchy of the patriarchal system, children rank at the bottom, beneath slaves and servants, beneath older children, beneath relatives, beneath mothers, beneath fathers.

Passages from the Hebrew Bible refer specifically to father-daughter incest. In Genesis 19:30-36, Lot's daughters conspire to lay with him in order to preserve his seed. "Come let us make our father drink wine, and we will lie with him that we may preserve offspring through him."[7] The responsibility for this action was placed clearly on Lot's daughters. Just as the practice of using children for sex has continued throughout history, so has the practice of accusing those children of seduction.

In order to determine whether the story of Lot and his daughters is about child sexual abuse or about father-daughter incest, a Hebrew Bible scholar would need to try and identify the ages of the daughters at the time of the sexual encounter, as well as the sociological definitions of adult and child. We do know the nameless daughters were physically capable of conceiving, and that while living in Sodom future husbands, referred to as "sons in law," had been chosen for them.

Susan Brownmiller indicates that ancient laws against father-daughter incest are stated clearly in the Code of Hammurabi. "A man who stole the virginity of another man's daughter might lawfully be killed. A man who 'knew' his own daughter was merely banished from the city."[8] The author of Genesis carefully explained that Lot was sent out of Sodom by God, and that he went into the hills because he was "afraid" to remain in Zo'ar. However, the information from the Code of Hammurabi, along with Lot's documented sexual relationship with his daughters, could cause one to wonder if this was the first and only sexual incident between father and daughters, and exactly why Lot left Zo'ar and dwelt in the hills.

Leviticus 18:6-18 begins, "None of you shall approach one near of kin to him to uncover nakedness. I am the LORD."[9] This passage continues with a long list of relatives one should avoid sexually. The passage is addressed to men, and although sex with a kinsman's daughter is forbidden, no prohibition regarding sex with one's own daughter is stated, "perhaps because a patriarch had to be recognized as owning the female members of his household."[10] Sex with male children could be prohibited by Leviticus 18:22, "You shall not lie with a male as a female," but just as daughters are not mentioned in the list, neither does it state specifically, "You shall not uncover the nakedness of your son."

Mosaic Law included injunctions against only what was considered "corruption" of children. "The penalty for sodomy with children over nine was death by stoning, but copulation with younger children was not considered a sexual act, and was punishable only by a whipping as a matter of public discipline."[11]

In 5th century B.C.E. Athens, pederastic relationships were common. "The archetype [Lover/Beloved] relationship was between a mature man at the height of his sexual power and need and a young, erotically-undeveloped boy just before puberty."[12] Sex between the Lover and Beloved was usually intercrural [the man inserted his penis between the boy's legs], and took place frontally since penetration from behind was regarded as humiliating. Anal sex was, however, used regularly as an initiation ritual into adult society.

> By subordinating his needs and desires to those of the older initiates, [the boy] learns to take his place in the power hierarchy of organized society. In time he will live to inflict the same humiliation on the next generation of novices.[13]

*Victims of victims of victims of victims of victims of . . .*

In the 4th century B.C.E., Plato had the idea that all children should be raised in common. Aristotle's objection "was that when men had sex with boys, they wouldn't know if they were their own sons, which would be 'most unseemly'."[14] This objection remained evident into the early days of the Christian movement. The Romans of the 1st century C.E. made an effort to protect free-born children from sexual abuse and punished this act severely. Abandoned children or children of slavery were, however, used freely for sex. The early Christians became disturbed about the possibility of accidental incest, worrying that a father, forgetting a child he abandoned, might accidently have intercourse with a son or a daughter.[15]

New Testament references to incest concern sexual activity with household members consistent with the property regulations of the Holiness Code. In 1st-century Israel, as well as the Greco-Roman world, ethical practices around sexuality were rooted in "the principle of respect for sexual property."[16] Incest [including sexual use of children] was considered a "violation of family hierarchy by arrogating to oneself a father's rights."[17] "Neither in the Hebrew Bible nor the New Testament does incest seem to be condemned for eugenic reasons."[18] There are no specific teachings against sex with children in the New Testament, but the Mosaic admonitions against corruption of children remain clear in Matthew 18:6 and Mark 9:42: "Whoever causes one of these little ones who believe in me to sin, it would be better for him if a great millstone were hung around his neck and he were thrown into the sea."[19]

In the 4th century C.E., St. Augustine wrote about his childhood.

I was severely beaten. For this procedure seemed wise to our ancestors; and many, passing the same way in the days past, had built a sorrowful road, by which we too must go, with multiplication of grief and toil upon the sons of Adam.[20]

Augustine, himself a victim of abuse as a school boy, contributed a justification for "hard and frequent punishments inflicted on the child" to the educational philosophy of early Christian theology.[21] And although Pope Leo the Great wrote positively about Christ's love for childhood,[22] it seems that Augustine's works "prepared the way for retaining under Christian auspices that sorrowful road . . . which he, as a child, had so much hated."[23] Although Augustine's abuse as a child does not specifically indicate sexual abuse, nor does his work in anyway advocate sexual abuse as a form of appropriate punishment, his message does lend credence to Roland Summit's theory of the intergenerational chain of child abuse.[24]

In biographies of many Irish saints, incest, as well as adultery, is commonly encountered.[25] Saint Dymphna, an incest victim living in 7th-century Ireland, left behind a tragic story. Dymphna was the daughter of a pagan Irish king and a Christian mother. After his wife died, the king desired his daughter Dymphna in marriage. Resisting him, Dymphna fled. The king found her and beheaded her.[26] In the 13th century, the body of St. Dymphna "was discovered in the Flemish town of Cheel near Antwerp, and a number of lunatics and epileptics were allegedly restored to health."[27] Because of this "miracle," Saint Dymphna became the patron saint of the mentally ill. Given the symptoms experienced by victims of child sexual abuse and adult survivors, it seems fitting, indeed, that an incest victim should be the patroness for people who are emotionally disturbed and psychologically distraught—lunatics? *victims of victims. . . ?*

In the 13th century, Saint Thomas Aquinas wrote on Sex and the Law of Nature, separating sexual sins into sins according to Nature and sins against Nature. He regards as less serious acts such as rape or incest [with a member of the opposite sex], which are physically complete.[28] Sexual sins against Nature, i.e., masturbation, homosexuality, and beastiality, carried a more serious penance, which was executed in public if the sins were considered an affront to members of the community.[29] Aquinas had no specific category or admonitions for sex with children.

Jean Gerson studied the sexual behavior of children for the benefit of confessors in the 15th century. In a sermon against lechery for the Fourth Sunday of Advent, Gerson warned the child to prevent others from "touching him or kissing him, and if he has failed to do so, he must report this in every instance in confession."[30] Memories of my early childhood confessions haunt me as I think of these 15th-century child penitents reporting the sexual violations against them. My confessions began with, "Bless me, Father, for *I have sinned* . . ." and ended with the Act of Contrition, "*Oh my God, I am heartily sorry for having offended thee* . . ." Surely, the child must have understood the responsibility and the offense for the touches belonged to him or her. Just as sexism and racism have become so ingrained in our speech and practices that we sometimes don't even realize or notice them, so has the concept of "guilty child" become accepted in our culture. Guilt and shame about the abuse they suffered are common feelings reported by victimized children as well as adult survivors.

In France in the early 17th century, Heroard, the physician for King Henry IV, kept a diary and carefully recorded details of Louis XIII's childhood. During Louis' "first three years, no one showed any reluctance or saw any harm in jokingly touching the child's sexual parts."[31] "When he was between five and six, people stopped talking about his sexual parts, while he started talking more about other people's."[32] By the time Louis was five, he reportedly instigated sexual activities with his nanny.[33]

In 1962, social historian Philippe Aries indicated that these practices were common in other families as well—nobles and commoners alike. In 1988, historian Lloyd DeMause took Aries to task. "It is the social historian, whose job it is to dig out the reality of social conditions in the past, who defends himself most vigorously against the facts he turns up."[34]

> Philippe Aries comes up with so much evidence of open sexual molesting of children that he admits that "playing with children's privy parts formed part of a widespread tradition;" he goes on to describe a traditional scene where a stranger throws himself on a little boy while ri-

ding in a train, "his hand brutally rummaging inside the child's fly," while the father smiled[35] . . . while the father roared with laughter.[36]

Aries argued that this scene, which occurred in the 20th-century, should help us to better understand and accept the moral behaviors of the 17th century. And then he continued with his horrifying defense of child sexual abuse.

All that was involved was a game whose scabrous nature we should beware of exaggerating: there was nothing more scabrous about it than there is about the racy stories men tell each other nowadays.[37]

Aries also provided his readers with his opinion about the effects of such sexual behavior on a child.

This lack of reserve with regard to children surprises us: we raise our eyebrows at the outspoken talk but even more at the bold gestures, the physical contacts about which it is easy to imagine what a modern psychoanalyst would say. The psychoanalyst would be wrong.[38]

A host of horrified voices gather in disagreement with Aries. Even though psychology had not yet been discovered in the 17th century, people still had psyches which were damaged by the early sexual abuse. They were *victims of victims of* . . .

In the 18th-century, the campaign against sexual abuse of children added a new dimension: "punishing the little boy or girl for touching its own genitals";[39] and the plague raged on because no one else was punished for touching the child's genitals. Francois Joachim de Pierre de Bernis, French cardinal and statesman, recalled being sexually molested by a nurse as a child. Out of his own experience he warned parents:

. . . nothing is so dangerous for morals and perhaps for health as to leave children too long under the care of chambermaids. . . They dare with a child that which they would be ashamed to risk with a young man.[40]

In Germany, one doctor reported that nursemaids and servants carried out "all sorts of sexual acts" on children "for fun."[41]

In 1896 "the connection between a history of childhood sexual trauma and psychological disturbance in adult life was first proposed by Sigmund Freud."[42] Female patients were diagnosed by Freud as suffering from hysteria; their symptoms included anxiety attacks, bodily disgust, mental sensitiveness, hyperactivity, crying spells, suicide attempts, and outbursts of despair.[43] Based on modern reports, not much has changed in this symptom pattern. Therefore, contrary to Aries' thinking, it would lead one to believe that since the manifestation of symptoms following childhood sexual abuse has remained the same for the 100 years after Freud's identification, the symptoms were much the same before Freud's identification.

Early in his career, Freud believed that his patients had, in fact, been sexually abused by adults during childhood. Most often the women named their fathers as their abusers; some of them men who were friends and colleagues of Freud. As a result of "repeated and persistent recrimination"[44] by his colleagues, Freud finally decided to consider reports by patients of early sexual abuse as female fantasy.[45]

Child sexual abuse continued into the 20th century in a way that is almost too horrifying to report. According to psychoanalyst Robert Fleiss, as late as 1900 "there were still people who believed venereal disease could be cured by means of sexual intercourse with children."[46]

In 1920, British author Virgina Woolf began the Memoirs Club, which was perhaps one of the first therapy groups for women. The women could share their writings with the group in safety and support. Woolf, who was sexually abused by her half-brother, George Duckworth, for 9 or 10 years, shared this story with her Club on November 17, 1920.

> George Duckworth had become after my mother's death, for all practical purposes the head of the family. It was usually said that he was father and mother, sister and brother in one—and all the old ladies of Kensington and Belgravia added with one accord that Heaven had blessed those poor Stephen girls beyond belief . . . Sleep had almost come to me. The room was dark. The house silent. Then, creaking stealthily, the door opened; treading gingerly, someone entered. "Who?" I cried. "Don't be frightened," George whispered, "And don't turn on the light, Oh Beloved, Beloved . . ." and he flung himself on my bed, and took me in his arms. Yes, the old ladies of Kensington and Belgravia never knew that George Duckworth was not only father and mother, brother and

sister to those poor Stephen girls; he was their lover also.[47]

George rationalized and explained his behavior as an attempt to comfort Virginia "for the fatal illness of [their] father."[48]

> Virtually every male member of the Stephen household was engaged in this [overt sexual assault, temper tantrum, physical violence, sexually threatening behavior, bullying, abductions, and probably even rape] behavior; without exception, all the women within the family were the victims of abuse or sexual violence.[49]

Virginia was often described as "mad" and committed suicide by drowning herself in 1941. Virginia Woolf "could not ever forget what had happened to her. She could never forget the betrayal of her childhood innocence and the consequences, which lasted a lifetime. Nor should we."[50] Nor should we forget the countless other *victims of victims of victims ...*

In 1948 Alfred Kinsey, zoology professor from Indiana University, published the results of his survey about human sexuality. *Sexual Behavior in the Human Female* indicated that 25% of the women responding to Kinsey's questionnaire said "they had either had sex with adult men while they were children or had been approached by men seeking sex."[51] These were startling statistics, but "even more remarkable was the degree to which that part of Kinsey's report was almost completely ignored, not just by the public but by his fellow researchers."[52]

The sexual abuse of children carries a long, painful, burdensome history of 5000 years. However, the taboo of listening to the victims, hearing their accounts and taking their pain seriously has been broken only for a short 20 years. In the late 1960s, female authors began to write about their experiences of childhood sexual abuse. In the late 1970s, professionals in the fields of social work, psychology and medicine began to pay closer attention to the issue. Swiss psychologist Alice Miller, a survivor of child abuse, was the first person to speak powerfully about the disrespect for and the abuse of children. With her groundbreaking work, Miller has identified how the impact of child abuse acted out in adult life has and will adversely effect our world.[53]

"The history of childhood is a nightmare from which we have only begun to awaken."[54] Professionals in the behavioral and social science fields have begun to pay attention to the children and the anguish of their abuse. But what about religious professionals and religious communities?

# CHAPTER FIVE

# *Ministries in Action: Responses by Religious Communities*

Education is the most powerful weapon you can use to change the world.
—Nelson Mandela, President, African National Congress

A true revolution of value will soon cause us to question the fairness and justice of many of our past policies . . . True compassion is more than flinging a coin to a beggar; it understands that an edifice which produces beggars needs restructuring.
—Martin Luther King, Jr., *Where Do We Go From Here?*

Compassion equals justice. You not only look after the wounded person on the road, but you go after the bandits so they don't do it again.
—Father Jon Sobrino, S.J.

## Jane

### *"We Are Not Alone . . ."*

My name is Jane. I'm 16 years old and a junior in high school. From the time I was a little girl, about 5 years old, I guess, my father was sexually abusing me. And until I saw a video at school in the 9th grade, I didn't even know it was "abuse." I always felt pretty weird about it, you know, scared, ashamed and sick to my stomach a lot, but Dad told me it was OK. It was "Good," he said, because I was "special," and he loved me "so much." Even though it hurt sometimes, I thought he was loving me, not abusing me.

And then I saw this video about sexual abuse in my Health Science class at school. I knew for sure, right then, that what my Dad was doing was wrong. I felt really confused, dirty and scared. Oh, I felt stupid, too. Stupid and mad at myself because I didn't know what was happening.

I didn't know what to do, but I just kept getting more and more upset inside. I was nervous all the time. I cried a lot and had headaches every single day. I was really tired because I was so nervous I couldn't sleep at night. I didn't want to talk to any of my friends or go to school anymore. But I did. I did everything as usual. I kept pretending, you know, like always, that everything in my life was just fine. It was the worst feeling.

I was truly confused. I didn't really want to tell Dad to stop because I didn't want to hurt his feelings, and I didn't know if he would stop anyway. I didn't want to tell him that I knew he was abusing me, and I especially didn't want him to think that I didn't love him anymore. Besides, what we did felt really good sometimes. I liked getting attention from my Dad. I was afraid to tell Mom because I didn't think she'd believe me, or if she did, I was afraid she would blame me.

I was afraid that nobody would believe me, and everyone would blame me. I was so scared all the time that finally I prayed to God to help me, just because I didn't know who else to ask.[1] ❖

# Daniel

## *"Pray For Us"*

Many times, facing the swollen amounts of emotion which had no where to go, I know I would have died if I had to face it alone. Without daily contemplation and meditation I slip back into the victim stance—where everything in the world that is wrong is my fault. It is only by daily contact with a concept of spirituality that this feeling of uselessness is removed.

I have found the principles of honesty and spirituality indispensable in discovering what I had been carrying around that wasn't mine. Without the concept of the universe being bigger than me, and its having some kind of plan, then I would not have been able to continue living.

Every time I deal with any part of my past I am attacked from within. The shatteredness of my soul is still fresh and without God I would die. It takes a whole lot of prayer to heal evil. If you do nothing else today, please don't forget to pray for us.[2] ❖

# Ministries in Action:
## Introduction

God, religion and religious communities play an enormously important role in the lives of the majority of Americans. In desperation, victims and survivors of child sexual abuse often turn to God and to their religious communities for assistance and comfort. How do these communities respond to the victims' direct pleas for help and/or their silent cries?

In an effort to determine responses, current interest and specific actions by religious communities concerning the issue of child sexual abuse, a telephone survey of two national organizations and eight religious denominations was conducted during January and February, 1991.

The national organizations contacted were: the National Council of Churches (NCC) in Washington, DC and The National Center for the Prevention of Child Abuse (NCPCA) in Chicago, IL. The General Board of the NCC adopted a Policy Statement on "Family Violence and Abuse" on November 14, 1990. Child sexual abuse is listed in the statement among a host of family problems, including physical and/or psychological assault, battering, mental rape, and destruction of property.[3] In an effort to encourage religious communities to observe *Child Abuse Prevention Month*, which has been designated as April, in a religious way, the NCPCA develops and provides annually a *Resource Packet for Religious Leaders on Child Abuse Prevention*. The primary goal of this effort is "to awaken members of religious communities to the pain and rejection that afflicts American children and their families."[4] The *Resource Packet* includes definitions, a brief introduction to the problem of child abuse—mentioning but not focusing on child sexual abuse—suggested activities for religious communities, and worship materials.

Denominations contacted during the original survey were: American Baptist, Episcopal, Lutheran, Presbyterian, Roman Catholic, Unitarian Universalist, United Church of Christ, and

United Methodist. In October 1992, follow-up information was obtained from five of the original denominations: Episcopal, Evangelical Lutheran and the Lutheran Church-Missouri Synod, Roman Catholic, Unitarian Universalist and United Church of Christ. In an attempt to avoid racial, cultural and socio-economic class differences and biases, mainly white, middle-class denominations were selected for the survey. Although much of the data was gathered through local and regional sources in Massachusetts and New England, an attempt was made to collect information on national programs as well as regional ones.

The organizational structures of the various denominations hindered or helped my ability to gather information directly and easily. I was often referred to a number of offices within one denomination before deciding to end my inquiry, either when reaching someone who could help me or who offered no information and no further contacts. The differences between the denominations governed by congregational polity, regional bishops/presidents, and/or those having one national office where programs were developed and disseminated to local congregations also affected my ability to obtain information.

As a result of the information collected by the survey, it was determined that, institutionally and locally, religious communities respond to the moral emergency of child sexual abuse in three general ways:

1. *Religious Education/Abuse Prevention:* These programs usually consist of Religious Education curricula, to be used in Sunday School settings, directed at a child population, ages 8-18.

2. *Social Justice:* The major social justice effort of the denominations contacted consists of resolutions passed at Annual Meetings/General Assemblies/Synods, etc. Usually, but not always, child sexual abuse is included, or assumed to be included, with the larger issues of domestic violence, child abuse, and/or child advocacy.

3. *Pastoral Care and Counseling:* These programs and efforts involve counseling and support services to victims, adult survivors, and their families. Several denominations did not mention any "official" pastoral response to child sexual abuse. However, it is presumed that most pastors, priests, rabbis and

other religious leaders in all religious communities will provide pastoral guidance to victims and survivors of child sexual abuse when the need arises.

Representatives of some denominations also directed me to organizations or pastors who provide "Focused Ministries" which include child sexual abuse as a part of other pastoral tasks or broader programs, or focus specifically on child sexual abuse.

## AMERICAN BAPTIST CHURCH (ABC)

RELIGIOUS EDUCATION/PREVENTION: In the Boston area, the American Baptist Church currently has no specific educational programming on child sexual abuse. In 1989, a sexuality program on AIDS was developed for junior and senior high school students. Nationally, the ABC offered special workshops at a recent conference for religious education professionals on family violence.

JUSTICE PROGRAMS: In 1985, the ABC passed a well-informed resolution which acknowledged their concern about the widespread and violent sexual abuse of children. However, no programming has followed the resolution.

## THE EPISCOPAL CHURCH

RELIGIOUS EDUCATION/PREVENTION: The Reverend Ann Franklin teaches courses for seminarians at the Episcopal Divinity School in Cambridge, Massachusetts on domestic and sexual violence. Her focus is woman-battering and father-daughter incest. Franklin was trained by Reverend Marie Marshall Fortune, a United Church of Christ minister and renowned specialist in the field of domestic and sexual violence. Following the training, it was Franklin's plan to teach other professionals in the Episcopal Church to lead workshops for parishes on these issues. Although she is eager to provide this training, Franklin indicated that there is not much call for her to do so.

In 1988, an Episcopal organization based in Boston, the Women in Crisis Committee, published perhaps the best resource available to aid ministers in responding to disclosure of child sexual abuse by victims and adult survivors. The brochure, *Responding to Incest: In Memory of Nancy*, has power in its very existence. It was published with money bequeathed to the Women in Crisis Committee by Nancy, an incest survivor who killed herself. The brochure was originally sent to all Episcopal bishops and is available upon request. Widespread distribution and use of this unique and valuable resource has not occurred within the Episcopal denomination.

The National Women in Ministry Department of the Episcopal Church regularly publishes articles on child sexual abuse in newsletters and magazines in an effort to educate through print media. Their concerted effort is admirable, and one particular resource, "S.A.R.A.H.," written by a survivor of child sexual abuse, is exceptional. However, there is not yet much follow-up with or interest by the clergy in this resource.

JUSTICE PROGRAMS: At their 69th General Convention in 1988, the Episcopal Church first passed resolutions citing child sexual abuse as a serious social problem deserving church attention. Since then, however, the Episcopal Church has, as have other denominations, placed considerable focus on the issue of clergy abuse. It was planned that this focus would include the abuse of children. It would not, however, specifically address the sexual abuse of children within American society.

The completed Clergy Abuse Program for the Episcopal Church appeared in the September, 1992 issue of the *Episcopal Times*. The program focuses completely on adult victims. There is no mention of children as victims or children as accusers. Specific training regarding this program was provided for clergy, and in the Boston Diocese attendance was mandatory.

In the fall of 1992, Dee Whyte, of the Massachusetts Children's Trust Fund, began discussing the possibility of developing programs to educate Episcopal clergy and other religious leaders about issues surrounding child abuse with Bishop Johnson of the Boston Diocese. According to Ms. Whyte, the Bishop is receptive to the idea. These programs would not be specific to child sexual abuse, but would include all forms of child abuse: emotional, physical, and sexual abuse, and neglect. The day-long training programs would include some important "basics": child abuse reporting laws and procedures, pastoral care, practical information regarding risk management and screening of individuals (volunteers and staff) for possible perpetrators, and developing written policy guidelines for reporting child abuse for their churches. According to Whyte, religious communities, as a whole, are a decade or two behind the school systems in developing and implementing clear, *written* policies specifically stating how and by whom disclosures made to church personnel would be reported.[5] Whyte hopes that Bishop Johnson will be as adamant about the importance of training the Episcopal clergy and religious leaders about the issue of child abuse as he was about the issue of clergy abuse. She hopes he will also make attendance at the child abuse trainings mandatory!

FOCUSED MINISTRIES:

1) *St. Andrew's Episcopal Church*
   *Framingham, MA*
   *Reverend Phil Jerauld, Associate Rector, and Nancy Jerauld*

In 1986, in response to the needs of two adult survivors of child sexual abuse, Reverend Phil and Nancy Jerauld and an adult survivor developed a one-day conference dealing specifically with the issue of child sexual abuse. The conference was held at St. Andrew's Episcopal Church. Survivors, therapists, teachers and ministers in the local area were invited to attend. The focus was "From Silence to Speech," stressing the importance of being able to talk about the issue. Follow-up conferences were offered again in 1987, "Breaking the Power of the Past: Men and Women Surviving Sexual Abuse," and in 1988, "Telling the Secret, Sharing the Experience, Changing the System."

In November of 1988, an on-going group of Incest Survivors Anonymous (ISA) began meeting weekly at St. Andrew's. 12-16 survivors have continued to meet regularly.

The original goal of St. Andrew's conferences was to create an on-going support group for survivors. Since this goal was met through the ISA group, the church did not continue with the annual child sexual abuse conference. However, St. Andrew's did donate their church facilities to "New England-ISA" for its 1991 conference, "Courageous Journey," which was held on April 27, 1991. Nancy and Phil Jerauld have since relocated to Maine. The ISA group continues to meet at St.

cated to Maine. The ISA group continues to meet at St. Andrew's Church.

### 2) St. James Episcopal Church
### Old Town, Maine
### Reverend Malcolm Burson, Rector

In 1983, a parishioner at St. James disclosed her history of child sexual abuse to Reverend Burson. In response to her sharing, Burson and the parishioners of St. James began an educational process into the area of child sexual abuse which resulted in a social ministry supported by the entire congregation.

In 1990 the story of their response, *Discerning the Call to Social Ministry*, was published by Alban Institute. This book demonstrates how one congregation became part of the solution to the problems of family violence and sexual abuse, instead of denying the existence of these painful issues within its midst.[6]

Although St. James Church does not currently offer educational programs to other congregations in the area of child sexual abuse, they have in the past, and would gladly do so again.

# THE EVANGELICAL LUTHERAN CHURCH IN AMERICA (ELCA)
# THE LUTHERAN CHURCH-MISSOURI SYNOD (LCMS)

RELIGIOUS EDUCATION/PREVENTION: In 1990, the Evangelical Lutheran Church in America funded six social ministry agencies across the country to provide training to clergy on domestic violence; child abuse and child sexual abuse were included. Unfortunately, funding was not available to expand or continue the program.

JUSTICE PROGRAMS: In early 1991, the Lutheran Church used their national publication, *Seeds for the Parish*, which is sent to 11,000 parishes, to bring "The Week of the Young Child" [celebrated in April] to the attention of Lutheran congregations. Parishes were strongly encouraged to obtain and use the "Religious Packet" offered by the NCPCA during Child Abuse Prevention Month: April 1991.

Also offered by the Lutheran Church sometime in 1991 was the 12-session social justice program for congregations entitled *OUR CHILDREN AT RISK: Hope For Our Future Together.* The program focuses on Peace, Justice and the Care of Creation. In the Justice section, specific attention is given to child abuse.

In 1991-1992 a Child Abuse Task Force was called together by the LCMS. In July 1992, the task force submitted a resolution with child abuse as the particular focus to the Annual Synod meeting, and have since begun to gather materials and develop programming around the issue.

PASTORAL CARE AND COUNSELING: The Lutheran Church recently surveyed the social service organizations affiliated with the ELCA and discovered that special programs in the area of domestic violence, including child abuse and child sexual abuse, were strongly needed. Following the survey, a reference guide was compiled so members of congregations could know of local agencies providing services specific to domestic violence. Furthermore, congregations were encouraged to display a poster indicating the types of services each agency offered, and their telephone numbers.

FOCUSED MINISTRY:

*COMMUNITY SEXUAL ABUSE PREVENTION PROGRAM (Formerly) SAFE KIDS PROGRAM: A Child Sexual Abuse Prevention Effort*
*Evangelical Lutheran Church of America (ELCA)*
*Cleveland, Ohio*
*Director: Debra D. Rossbach, M.S.*

The Safe Kids Program, sponsored by the Lutheran Metropolitan Ministry Association in Cleveland, Ohio, is one of the most comprehensive church-sponsored programs in the country focusing on the issue of child sexual abuse.

Safe Kids began in 1984 as a result of a specific incident of child sexual abuse presented to a Lutheran pastor in Cleveland. A major objective of the Safe Kids Program is to educate parents, school personnel and children—in that order—affiliated with Lutheran schools, about the issue of child sexual abuse. Between 1984 and 1990, 1,880 adults and 5,500 children in northeast Ohio area participated in the educational programming.

Although education in the Lutheran schools remains a central focus for the Safe Kids Program, it is by no means the only focus. Safe Kids has become a valuable resource on child sexual abuse, and provides exceptional reference guides for clergy, parents and school personnel. Statistics, definitions, facts, Ohio child abuse laws, intervention procedures, local resources, and a bibliography and readings specific to the particular user (i.e., teacher, pastor, parent) are included in the reference guides. Safe Kids also publishes and distributes an informative newsletter several times a year.

During October and November, 1990, Safe Kids offered six 1-day conferences for Lutheran clergy in northeast Ohio on child sexual abuse and domestic violence. Ms. Rossbach recommended that these conferences be viewed as the beginning of an on-going learning process for clergy rather than as a one-time opportunity. She further recommended that the ELCA require and support—on a national, synod and conference level—introductory educational programs on domestic violence and child sexual abuse in Lutheran seminaries.

In 1991, Safe Kids received a grant from the LCMS to expand the 1-day conferences for clergy throughout the state of Ohio. During October and November of 1991, Ms. Rossbach conducted training programs in five regions, covering all of Ohio. Again, she recommended that these conferences be viewed as the beginning of on-going trainings. And although no one has disagreed with Ms. Rossbach's recommendation, no one has actually supported the idea either. There has been no forthcoming sign of commitment to further clergy training on the issues of domestic violence and child sexual abuse in ways that matter: time, staff and funding. Ms. Rossbach received no subsequent grants to implement her proposed "on-going" learning process.

In 1986, Safe Kids received funding from the LCMS to develop and implement a pilot social justice project on child sexual abuse in 30 Cleveland area congregations; 15 congregations would participate in Phase One, and then following program revisions, 15 congregations would participate in Phase Two.

The project did not proceed according to plan. Although 11 congregations participated in Phase One for 21 months, instead of the suggested 6 months, none of them completed the project. Ms. Rossbach explained:

> All of the groups supported the initial premise of the need for education and awareness about child sexual abuse. However, there are no plans to develop an ongoing and active ministry in response to this issue in any of the participating groups. Even with the step-by-step details of a guidebook and available consultation from Safe Kids, the flaw in the concept of this pilot project seems to be the lack of a person/coordinator/organizer whose commitment is to this issue . . . This highly emotional and difficult issue seems to need a "leader" with a personal and/or driving commitment to a ministry involving child sexual abuse . . . to push this issue as an area needing church attention.[7]

Because of a trademark issue, The Safe Kids Program changed its name to Community Sexual Abuse Prevention Program in May of 1991. Although sexual abuse of children is—and always has been—the primary focus of the program, there has been resistance to the new name because it publicly identifies its focus. Rossbach is pleased with the new name. She believes it is a step forward to actually calling the program what it is: an effort in preventing sexual abuse.

## THE PRESBYTERIAN CHURCH U.S.A.

RELIGIOUS EDUCATION/PREVENTION: The National Religious Education Department of The Presbyterian Church, USA recently received a request from their General Assembly to develop a sex education program for elementary school children that will include a unit on sexual abuse. Although the department has received the request, they currently have no funding to create the program.

JUSTICE PROGRAMS: The Child Advocacy Department of the Presbyterian Church received a $100,000 grant from their own bicentennial Fund to develop model programs for training child-care workers in identifying child abuse. In 1991, $5000 of this grant will be available for use. This program has taken a back seat, however, to the larger effort of Child Advocacy funded with $330,000 in 1990. The major focus of the advocacy program is service, education and organizing in the areas of legislation and public policy.

# THE ROMAN CATHOLIC CHURCH

RELIGIOUS EDUCATION/PREVENTION: In the Boston Archdiocese, the Roman Catholic Church has not developed specific educational materials on child sexual abuse. When organizations sponsored by Catholic Charities provide educational programs, they use materials produced by The Judge Baker Children's Center in Boston or The Massachusetts Society for the Prevention of Cruelty to Children.

Currently, the national education department for the American Roman Catholic Church, which is located in Washington, DC, has no materials on child sexual abuse.

JUSTICE PROGRAMS: Although the Domestic and Social Development Department of the Roman Catholic Church in America does not specifically address the issue of child sexual abuse, they recently developed programs on domestic violence. Currently, they are working on pastoral response and education regarding drug abuse.

Because of the enormous publicity in recent years surrounding the accusations of child molestation against priests, the Roman Catholic Church has been preoccupied with the issue of clergy sexual misconduct with minors. Although the focus of my survey was not on the religious communities' responses to clergy abuse, I think it is important to acknowledge some of the ways the Catholic Church has recently, courageously, addressed the sexual abuse of children by priests, especially because their past responses have been less than admirable. Current efforts of the Roman Catholic Church are groundbreaking, and their methods can effectively serve as models for all religious communities, not just in addressing clergy abuse, but as models for the ways religious communities can acknowledge and respond to child sexual abuse within society as a whole.

The most comprehensive and impressive actions in this regard are: the report released in June 1992 by the Canadian Bishops' Ad Hoc Committee on Child Sexual Abuse, and the policy on Clerical Sexual Misconduct with Minors, established by the Archdiocese of Chicago in September 1992. The Canadian Report, "From Pain to Hope," states the clear intent to widen the perspective of their program from church to society. Although most of the recommendations of the report are concerned specifically with the sexual abuse of children by priests, the Canadian bishops urge the extensive cooperation of all Catholics regarding this moral emergency. "In our minds, our church would be socially irresponsible if it participated in the fight against child sexual abuse only when one of its ministers is implicated."[8] The Chicago Policy also focuses on the sexual abuse of children by priests; however many of its points reach beyond the walls of the Catholic Church in important ways. Both the Canadian Program and the Chicago Policy are highlighted briefly as "Focused Ministries."

PASTORAL CARE AND COUNSELING: The Roman Catholic Church approaches child sexual abuse as a dysfunctional family issue by offering counseling to child victims and adult survivors of child sexual abuse. In Massachusetts, six regional offices of Catholic Charities provide over 40 different kinds of services, depending upon the needs of particular communities. In the area of child sexual abuse, Catholic Charities provides counseling services, to victims referred by the Department of Social Services, offers individual and group therapy for adult survivors, and does outreach counseling in Catholic schools. A representative of one agency sponsored by the Catholic Church indicated the absence of, but the need for, counseling programs for offenders who are actively abusing children, but seeking help to stop.

Separate from pastoral care and counseling in the Roman Catholic Church is the profession of "spiritual direction." Spiritual directors are priests, nuns and laypersons, and they most often provide guidance in cooperation with retreat houses, parishes and seminaries. In their work, more and more spiritual directors are encountering more and more adults who have been sexually abused as children.

This issue is discussed so much more often—now—in both counseling and spiritual direction than it was even 10 or 15 years ago, and the spiritual directors and pastoral counselors are helping to create a climate of awareness within the Roman Church. They are the individuals who hear about—and experience first-hand—what sexual abuse in childhood does to people. Thus, with this first-hand experience, spiritual directors and pastoral counselors are the group most pre-disposed to create a climate that will insist on prevention.[9]

"From Pain to Hope," the Canadian Report, includes a detailed section on pastoral care for the victims of child sexual abuse. The Report stresses the importance of this type of care by acknowledging that the "wound inflicted by sexual abuse cuts much deeper than a physical wound," that "wounds such as these damage children to the very core of their being and their fundamental self-identity," and that the consequences of childhood abuse may continue to "trouble" the person even into adulthood.[10]

FOCUSED MINISTRIES:

1) *THE CHICAGO POLICY:* *"Clerical Sexual Misconduct With Minors: Policies for Education, Prevention, Assistance to Victims and Procedures for Determination of Fitness for Ministry."*

In his letter to Chicago Catholics, Cardinal Joseph Bernardin, Archbishop of Chicago, stresses two points:

- Sexual misconduct is wrong and will not be tolerated.

- As a church we must support and care for those who have been injured.[11]

These two points need not necessarily speak only about sexual misconduct "within" religious communities, generally, or the Catholic Church, specifically. This message is applicable and pertinent beyond the walls of the religious community: The sexual abuse of children is wrong. It isn't "more wrong" or "less wrong" when a Catholic priest is the abuser. It is just "wrong." As religious leaders, as a society, this message regarding child sexual abuse could be our credo: *the sexual abuse of children will not be tolerated.*

Cardinal Bernardin's Chicago Policy goes beyond just words, and this also adds to the policy's uniqueness. Article 1.2 addresses "Funding, staff and facilities." Only 21 words long, Article 1.2 is perhaps the lifeblood of the Policy and makes the unequivocal statement that Cardinal Bernardin is *serious*. Unlike some of the other denominations surveyed, which passed resolutions and requested programs but provided no funding, the Chicago Policy ensures "sufficient funding, staff and facilities to assure the effective implementation of the programs established by these provisions."[12]

Another important and widely applicable aspect of the Chicago Policy calls for "appropriate educational programs for seminarians and priests about the nature and effect of sexual misconduct with minors."[13] The archdiocese will take responsibility for the review and enhancement of existing courses on sexuality and sexual misconduct. Previously, very little sexual education took place in the formation of priests. As standard, a one semester course on sexual morality was required. This course focused on issues of sexual orientation, abortion, contraception, masturbation, and premarital sex from the perspective of counseling others. Child sexual abuse was not a topic of discussion.[14] The addition of "age-appropriate courses and components that deal in depth with psychological development, including both moral and deviant sexual behavior"[15] represents a major change in the formation of Roman Catholic clergy. Hopefully, this educational change will serve as a model for ALL denominations and ALL seminaries and institutions providing training to religious professionals.

The Chicago Policy also addresses the needs of victims. It provides for a toll-free hotline to handle complaints, a victim assistance minister, and assures that all allegations will be reported to the Illinois state agency handling child abuse cases. Diocesan personnel are expected to "cooperate with the civil authorities [and] comply with legally established reporting requirements."[16] Priests accused of sexual misconduct with minors will not be allowed to return to parish ministry or to a ministry which provides them access to children. They may not be allowed to return to ministry at all.

Cardinal Joseph Bernardin expressed sincere concern for the past victims of child sexual abuse, "I share the anguish of all those affected by this tragedy: the victims, their families, their communities and priests. While I cannot change the past I can do something about the future."[17] Cardinal Bernardin has learned from the past and he is taking steps to prevent the past from repeating itself in the future—in regard to the abuse perpetrated by pedophile and ephebophile priests. However, this is not the only type of child sexual abuse needing to be addressed by the Roman Catholic Church. Hopefully, the Chicago Policy will serve to assist and protect the larger community of child sexual abuse victims and survivors as well.

### 2) "FROM PAIN TO HOPE"
*Fifty Recommendations: The Church and Child Sexual Abuse*
*The Canadian Bishops' Ad Hoc Committee on Child Sexual Abuse*

The Canadian Report acknowledges the psychological, institutional, and social complexities surrounding the causes and the pervasive continuation of child sexual abuse in North American societies. This report expresses the "firm conviction that the concerted effort of many people will be needed to stem the tide of sexual abuse against children,"[18] and invites the Catholic brothers and sisters of Canada to address and respond to child sexual abuse in several ways:

- To move beyond the fear and shame surrounding the issue of child sexual abuse

- To break the silence

- To become actively involved in addressing and eradicating this "social affliction"

- To support the victims and survivors who, with great difficulty, struggle to allow a painful truth to be heard despite the conspiracy of silence

- To become informed about the child sexual abuse reporting laws and procedures, as well as education and prevention programs.[19]

"From Pain to Hope" also addresses the formation of seminarians, as well as the on-going education of priests. Proposed changes to the formation program are extensive; however, those applicable to the general issue of child sexual abuse include education of seminarians and in-depth counseling and spiritual direction.[20] Some suggestions for the continuing education of priests include "regular opportunities" for updating their knowledge through seminars which address child sexual abuse from three angles:

- New scientific knowledge, which would include current statistical and psychological data

- Church policy as well as civil and criminal laws

- Issues concerning moral theology, professional ethics and the theology of sexuality.[21]

The Canadian Report also calls for the "immediate and continuing research in the social sciences regarding the complex reality of human sexuality."[22]

The Bishops' committee stressed the point that their recommendations tried to reconcile the issue of child sexual abuse and the Church's response from the *two perspectives* which they considered "essential" in order for their report to be considered adequate: "compassion and responsibility."[23] I am reminded, here, of the ethicist and the prosecutor!

# THE UNITARIAN UNIVERSALIST ASSOCIATION (UUA)

RELIGIOUS EDUCATION/PREVENTION: In 1989, in response to a resolution on child abuse passed at the 1985 General Assembly, the UUA decided to add a unit on sexual abuse to the junior high school curriculum, *About Your Sexuality* (AYS). As development of the unit progressed, it was expanded into a separate curriculum, *About Sexual Abuse* (ASA), to be used in conjunction with AYS or *Life Issues For Teenagers*. Although ASA was designed for older teenagers, it can be adapted for older (adult) or younger populations.

At the 1989 and 1990 UUA General Assemblies, brief workshops were offered for clergy and church representatives on the specific issue of child sexual abuse.

Due to specific incidents of clergy sexual misconduct occurring in 1991, the UUA instigated training for clergy on this issue. A Task Force was developed and training around the country was provided by Reverend Marie Marshall Fortune. This program is not specific to the sexual abuse of children, but because one of the UU ministers investigated for sexual misconduct in the fall of 1991 was prosecuted and convicted of raping and sexually assaulting teen-age girls, including the abuse of children in the clergy abuse training was of primary concern.

Reverend Lucinda Duncan, Minister of Religious Education at The First Parish in Cambridge, who is also a regional trainer for the clergy sexual misconduct program, took her responsibilities to protect the children seriously and brought the issue to the forefront in her own church. The Religious Education Committee at First Parish asked every person working with children or youth to review the program expectations and to sign a code of ethics, "because safety of our children and youth is our absolute top priority."[24] According to Reverend Duncan, this action received positive responses both from volunteer teachers who are pleased that their work is being taken seriously, and from the parents who felt a sense of relief and pride that *their* church was taking a leadership role in protecting the children.[25]

JUSTICE PROGRAMS: In 1977, the Unitarian Universalist Association's General Assembly passed a resolution stating that child abuse and neglect were familial and societal problems of "national significance"; in 1985, child sexual abuse was resolved to be an immoral and unethical "continental problem."[26]

In 1989, the Unitarian Universalist Service Committee (UUSC) published *Promise The Children: A Guide for UU (Unitarian Universalist) Congregations to Focus on the Rights and Needs of Children in the US*. Although *Promise The Children* stresses the rights and needs of children as a "moral imperative," the moral emergency of child sexual abuse is conspicuous in its absence from the program. But perhaps the absence is actually in the minds and hearts of some of the UU religious community. During 1987 and 1988, with the responsibility for developing a program for children, the UUSC surveyed Directors of Religious Education, UU ministers and members of the Service Committee regarding their concerns. The returned surveys indicated interests in poverty, homelessness, child care, housing discrimination, and education. Since child sexual abuse—or child abuse in general—did not appear as an issue of religious concern for the population surveyed, it was not included in *Promise the Children.*[27]

## FOCUSED MINISTRY:

*Unitarian Universalist Fellowship*
*Lafayette, Indiana*
*Reverend Libbie Stoddard*

Reverend Stoddard's interest in child sexual abuse began in 1984 when a Unitarian Universalist minister serving a midwestern church was prosecuted and convicted of child sexual abuse. It was a shock to everyone, especially his ministerial colleagues, because he was a "nice, gentle, literate man."[28] The District UUA ministers met to support one another and agreed they would "do something" about the issue of child sexual abuse. And Reverend Stoddard has followed through with that agreement.

In 1985 Stoddard gave a sermon on child sexual abuse at the parish where she was and is the pastor. Subsequently, a woman in her congregation, who is a survivor, came forward and asked if there were any local support groups for survivors of child sexual abuse. Since there were no groups, Stoddard and the survivor started one. This on-going, monthly support group for adult female survivors of child sexual abuse has met regularly at the Unitarian Universalist Fellowship since 1986. The group, which is co-led by Reverend Stoddard and a local therapist, is provided to survivors free. The group meetings take place at the church. The space and cost of utilities is graciously provided by the congregation of the Unitarian Universalist Fellowship. The number of participants in the group, which began with a "drop in" format, ranged from 8 to 13. But, by the summer of 1992, so many women had been coming regularly to the group that they had to institute a waiting list. The group also expressed an interest in meeting more often than once a month, so they now meet bi-weekly. In the fall of 1992, the group published the first issue of their newsletter, *Speaking Out in Solidarity*, which was distributed to survivors in the surrounding area.

Since Stoddard began her focused ministry in the area of child sexual abuse, her work has expanded. She has developed and started groups for college students at nearby Purdue University, initiated support groups for professionals working with abuse survivors, and provided training for medical professionals at local hospitals. Stoddard's commitment to "doing something" about child sexual abuse is obvious and admirable. She has done all of this in addition to her regular duties as pastor of the Unitarian Universalist Fellowship.

In 1988, Reverend Stoddard wrote another sermon on child sexual abuse entitled "Not in My Family: Some Issues of Sexual Abuse." This challenging sermon, which went beyond the safety zone of just presenting information to actually acknowledging that members of her congregation may have sexually abused a child, was awarded the 1989 Clarence Skinner Sermon Award for social ministry by the Unitarian Universalist Association.

## THE UNITED CHURCH OF CHRIST (UCC)

RELIGIOUS EDUCATION/PREVENTION: The United Church of Christ offers two religious education curricula specifically on child sexual abuse:

1. *Preventing Sexual Abuse*, by Kathryn Goerig Reid and Marie Fortune, is a 13-session program about sexual abuse and prevention. It was written specifically for children, ages 9-12.

2. *Sexual Abuse Prevention: A Study for Teenagers*, by Marie Fortune, is a 5-session course for teenagers.

Currently being field-tested by the UCC is a progressive religious education program entitled, *Created in God's Image: A Sexuality Program for Ministry and Mission.* This program attempts to integrate human sexuality into the ministry and mission of the Church. The curriculum intends to deal with sexuality in a way that prevents abuse before it starts. *Created in God's Image* is designed for very young elementary school children.

JUSTICE PROGRAMS: At the 1991 General Meeting, the United Church of Christ is expected to vote on resolutions regarding the ethical conduct and sexual behavior of clergy.

These resolutions will include the abuse of children; however, they are not specific to children but to clergy.

While conducting my survey in 1991, I was referred to Reverend Ronald H. McLean, Associate Conference Minister for Mission Development and Social Responsibility of the Massachusetts conference. He listened intently as I explained the purpose of my survey. When I asked what the UCC Social Responsibility Department was doing about child sexual abuse, McLean replied, "Well, we're not doing anything, but maybe we should be."

And now, the Massachusetts conference is doing something about child sexual abuse. By June of 1991, McLean had called together a group of people from across the state to participate as members of the newly-formed Women and Children's Task force. This Task Force chose to address the issue of child sexual abuse as its first project.

In June of 1992, a resolution on "Ending the Silence and Breaking the Cycle of Child Sexual Abuse" was presented at the annual meeting of the Massachusetts Conference. This resolution calls for the education of all religious professionals concerning the devastating and long-lasting effects of child sexual abuse, encourages pastors to address the problem of child sexual abuse from the pulpit, and requests members of the congregations of the UCC to inform the Governor, the Department of Social Services, and the Attorney General that crimes against our children can no longer be tolerated.

The Task Force followed up on the resolution, which passed with overwhelming support from the 800 delegates attending the conference. Between January and April 1993, a day-long workshop inviting religious leaders "to hear" about child sexual abuse will be offered in six different regions throughout the state. In October 1993, the Task Force will co-sponsor, along with Harvard Divinity School, a multi-disciplinary inter-religious conference on Child Sexual Abuse. Speakers will include the local district attorney, a child psychiatrist, a seminary professor, social services representatives, a bureau chief of victim witness services, and many ministers.

The idea of offering a healing retreat for survivors of child sexual abuse and specific training in pastoral care and counseling are being considered as future projects. Currently, other ideas for future programming are being gathered from within the UCC community. Based on ideas already collected, it appears that the interests and needs surrounding the issue of child sexual abuse are vast and varied.

PASTORAL CARE AND COUNSELING: The UCC offers a book to aid clergy in advising victims of domestic violence and sexual abuse of their legal rights. The book, written by Mary S. Winters, J.D., is entitled *Laws Against Sexual and Domestic Violence.* The Center for the Prevention of Sexual and Domestic Violence in Seattle, Washington offers an important videotape, *Hear Their Cries: Religious Responses to Child Abuse.* This 48-minute documentary addresses the role of clergy and lay leaders in preventing child abuse.

FOCUSED MINISTRY:

*The Center for the Prevention of Sexual and Domestic Violence
Seattle, Washington
Reverend Marie Marshall Fortune, Director*

In 1976—the date is noteworthy because it represents and stresses the innovative nature of this program—Reverend Marie Fortune founded The Center for the Prevention of Sexual and Domestic Violence. Fortune's interest in developing this center resulted from her discovery that Seattle clergy didn't even know how or where to refer a woman who had been the victim of domestic violence. Her goal was to change that situation—immediately—and begin providing services to women and children.[29] The work of The Center has continued since 1976 and now offers training for clergy, nationwide, on family violence. Their work includes child sexual abuse among the other domestic violence issues. Fortune also offers trainings on clergy abuse, which includes the sexual abuse of children by clergy.

## THE UNITED METHODIST CHURCH

RELIGIOUS EDUCATION/PREVENTION: The United Methodist Church recommends the UCC Curriculum, *Sexual Abuse Prevention: A Study for Teenagers,* by Marie Fortune, for use in their church schools. In the Boston region, one-day training workshops on sexual abuse are occasionally offered for clergy.

JUSTICE PROGRAMS: The General Board of Global Ministries of the United Methodist Church has done extensive work regarding crises affecting women and children. In 1988 they launched an initiative in the general area of "women and families," and have produced some exceptional materials:

1. *Children and Youth in Jeopardy*, by Carol D. Allman and Peggy L. Halsey, was shared nationally with United Methodist congregations. Although child sexual abuse does not appear in the table of contents as an issue, one page on child sexual abuse can be located in the booklet under the heading, "Child Neglect and Abuse, Both Physical and Emotional." References to child sexual abuse are also found under "Teen Suicide" and "Teenage Prostitution."

2. "Denial will not make Child Abuse Disappear," an article by Beverly Jackson, Director of the Department of Welfare for the United Methodist Board of Church and Society, was written in 1982 and currently remains in publication.

3. *Abuse in the Family: Breaking the Church's Silence*, written in 1984 by Peggy Halsey was revised in 1990. Some objectives of this program are:

- To recognize family violence as a major social problem

- To examine the extent and roots of the Church's silence on issues of physical and sexual abuse within families

- To expose cultural and religious beliefs which support family violence and suggest ways to re-learn healthier behaviors.[30]

PASTORAL CARE AND COUNSELING: In 1984, The United Methodist Church began to sponsor a special Pastoral Ministry to runaway children.

# Ministries in Action:
## Summary

Nelson Mandela, President of the African National Congress, is convinced that education can change the world. But in the area of child sexual abuse, this essential question remains: Who is being educated? The majority of educational programs sponsored by religious communities focus on educating the children—the victims—to protect themselves. By asking and expecting our children—these small, vulnerable and precious human beings who have not yet reached the age of majority or the age of consent, or perhaps not even the age of reason—to protect themselves, we are also asking them to be responsible for repairing a part of the broken world—that they did not break—long before that world becomes theirs.

A few of the denominations surveyed in 1991 had made a minimal effort to educate clergy and seminarians about child sexual abuse; even fewer had attempted to educate their congregations. But in order to begin dismantling the destructive myths surrounding child sexual abuse and to begin making a difference, adults *must be* educated about the severity of the problem and about the serious consequences. Since adults are the perpetrators, only they possess the power to end the abuse.

Justice programs sponsored by the religious communities surveyed acknowledge the existence of child sexual abuse and consider it a serious issue. However, most programs include child sexual abuse within the broader issues of domestic violence and/or child abuse. Despite these admirable efforts and the best of intentions, when child sexual abuse is included with other social concerns, another opportunity for denial is offered. The combining of issues allows people to keep that which is "too cruel for mind and memory to face,"[31] hidden in the shadows. Child sexual abuse is an issue of social and religious concern that needs to be swept out from underneath the rug and put in the spotlight in order for change to occur. If religious communities truly want to address the problem of child sexual abuse, a singular, deliberate focus on the issue is necessary.

Pastoral care and counseling are essential religious responses to victims and survivors of child sexual abuse and their families. Continuing and increasing support of these programs is important. Long-term psychotherapy is often the treatment of choice for victims of child sexual abuse. Individual and group therapy can be effective methods of individual healing, and could even deter future abuse. However, therapy and counseling offer solutions only on an individual basis, only to a few people, and therefore cannot be expected to have a major impact on a systemic problem that affects *millions* of people. Prevention is the preferred approach. Education of religious adults is my recommended method for beginning the prevention effort.

The focused ministries popped up around the country following the courageous and caring responses of particular ministers to specific encounters with child sexual abuse. These are admirable ministries, but again, they offer only individual solutions to a systemic problem. Entire institutions—not just isolated ministers and parishes, or one conference here and another synod there—need to address the issue of child sexual abuse before any transformation of consciousness can even begin to occur.

At present, the issue of clergy abuse seems to be HIGH on the list of concerns for most religious organizations. Surely these concerns are rooted in moral and ethical standards as well as true pastoral support of the victims. However, the reality of legal responsibility and civil action against the offending clergy and religious communities cannot be denied. Organized religious communities MUST focus their attention on clergy misconduct because they are being sued for damages. The potential lawsuits against the Roman Catholic priests, alone, could result in billions of dollars.

> Between 1983 and 1988, 140 priests and brothers have been reported for sexual involvement with children nationwide. Approximately 95 of these cases entered the civil or criminal arena. In 8 states, involving 13 priests, $16.8 million was paid to 36 victims and their families.[32]

In 1988 insurance companies discontinued their coverage for charges of sexual abuse for diocesan personnel, "making the Church even more vulnerable."[33]

Some have suggested that the celibacy of Roman Catholic priests has contributed to the problem of child sexual abuse. If only they were married, if only they had families, the pedophile and ephebophile priests wouldn't need to take the risk or make the effort to sexually abuse children within their parishes. Married clergy from other religious communities also sexually abuse children. Sometimes the children of relatives or friends or neighbors, but most often, their own. Married priests with a tendency toward pedophilia or ephebophilia could therefore keep child sexual abuse within their own homes and out of the parishes. Would this be an improvement, or merely a means of shifting the problem from the church to the home?

As a practical measure, the religious communities are focusing their efforts on clergy sexual misconduct. And it is an important focus. However, the use of power by religious leaders to sexually abuse children (and vulnerable adults) underscores the prevalence of the misuse of power in our society. The sexual abuse of children is not a problem inherent in the structure of religious communities. This is a problem inherent in our homes, our schools, our social systems, our society, our lives. People who sexually molest children are drawn to work with vulnerable populations, so the religious communities are popular targets. However, they are not the only targets. In the midst of this flurry of education in the area of clergy abuse, let us not forget that 42% of the victims of child sexual abuse are molested in their own homes by *biological* relatives. That percentage increases to 60% when abusers from within step families, foster families and adoptive families are included.[34]

# CHAPTER SIX

# *An Invitation to Speak, to Hear, to Act: A Program for Prophetic Ministry*

> My pledge to the children . . . While I cannot change the past, I can do something about the future. We stand accountable, and are able to model to ourselves and to society at large how best to address these tragedies in the future.
>
> —Cardinal Joseph Bernardin

## An Invitation to Hear

Although the personal accounts of survivors of child sexual abuse have set the tone for the information following in each previous chapter, I feel that a brief introduction to the three personal accounts in Chapter Six would be helpful. I introduce the accounts of Nancy, Lee and Terri carefully, in order to prevent any misunderstandings.

The 1992 resolution passed by the Lutheran Church-Missouri Synod acknowledges that child sexual abuse can be "a definite hindrance to a child's faith."[1] Through their personal accounts, Nancy, Lee and Terri lift up some of the issues of faith and theology which are challenged by sexual abuse in childhood.

As a victimized child, Nancy prays in desperation to God, whom she understands to be "Almighty." When her prayers are not answered by God, she believes it is because she is guilty and deserves punishment. Only this conclusion makes sense to any child who has faith in Almighty God. As an adult, the anger Nancy feels about the injustice of the situation and the betrayal within her family lingers and continues to hurt her.

Lee's account may be especially challenging to the Christian readers. Searching for meaning in her life and her experience with "The Father," Lee rewrites one of the most revered Christian scriptures, Luke 1:26-36, the Annunciation and Mary's visit to Elizabeth. In doing so, she finds acceptance for herself within herself, but will Christian communities accept her? Will they understand her message, her plea for love and acceptance? Or will her radical approach leave her feeling abandoned once again? First, Lee was betrayed and abandoned by "The Father." Will she again be betrayed and abandoned by the religious community for expressing her secret in such a creative and self-loving way?

Terri's account challenges the concept of "Forgiveness." In the past, religious communities have stressed forgiveness. Some psychologists have even stressed forgiveness as a component necessary for healing. Linda, a survivor whose account appears in Chapter Seven, felt that she wasn't a good Christian— wasn't a good person—because she couldn't forgive her abuser. But current research, religious and secular, caution religious communities against hurrying victims and survivors to forgive the people who sexually abused them in childhood. As Terri informs us, some abusers don't apologize, don't ask to be forgiven. The Canadian Catholic Bishops have taken a bold stand on forgiveness, and their position supports Terri. We should not "demand premature forgiveness on the part of victims, particularly as a means of more or less silencing the demand of justice or concealing an unhealed wound."[2] Forgiveness is, by definition, a feeling, and it therefore arises spontaneously in response to a set of circumstances. Victims and survivors cannot "choose to forgive"; however, they can choose to be open to receiving the feeling of forgiveness. A lot can be learned from listening to the survivors. They will inform us about their positions on this theological issue. Most importantly, religious communities need to help victims and survivors to forgive *themselves*.

Nancy, Lee, Terri and Linda are wonderful women. They are struggling with life and healing. They are struggling with religious norms and practices that they don't seem to understand or to fit into. The challenge to religious Americans is to reach out and embrace these wonderful survivors who don't quite fit the mold. We need to understand that they don't fit—not necessarily by choice—but they don't fit because their life experiences have shaped them differently. The irony is just this: They don't fit, but they still want desperately to fit, to belong, to be loved and accepted even though their ideas and bodies may seem misshapen to some. In context, their thoughts and shapes make perfect sense. These wonderful people need to belong. They deserve to belong.

## Nancy

### "Using the Incest"

On November 28, 1984, I told my mother about my father's abuse, and she indicated a day or so later that she "couldn't deal with it, it's too close to Christmas."

Christmas, 1984. My siblings who didn't know about the abuse were very angry with me for not coming to my mother's. Another sister, who had known about the abuse for years, came to my house and criticized me for "carrying grudges" and for "taking it out on my mother."

I was angry at being made the villain of the situation, and I called my mother a few days later to ask why some explanation hadn't been made to my brother and sister so that they would understand why I wasn't at her house for Christmas. (I wasn't invited!) My mother's response was that I was being treated like the villain because I *was* the villain, both because I didn't tell her sooner, and because I told her now. "You should have told me sooner, or you should have kept your mouth shut."

During this conversation she also told me that I had been "using the incest" all my life, insinuating "to my benefit." This outrageous comment was so impossible for my rational mind to accept, for any rational mind, I'm sure, that I responded to my mother with complete sarcasm.

Oh, I used it all right. I used it to create amnesia. I wanted to block out most of the first nine years of my life. I didn't want to go through all these adult years with all those extra memories that I probably don't need. I used the incest to save space in my brain for more pleasant memories.

I used it to develop bad eye sight. Glasses helped cover my face and to cover the shame I felt about the awful things my father did to me.

And I used it to have something to pray about. PLEASE GOD, MAKE HIM STOP!

I used it to believe I was guilty of something and God wasn't going to make it stop because I *deserved* to be punished. And the incest *was* punishment

I used it to give my life meaning. It was my job to provide sexual satisfaction to my father so he wouldn't yell at everyone all the time. It was my job to keep the family together. If I didn't "put out" he'd leave. Or he'd go to prostitutes. We'd be poor. Have no money for food. It made me feel important.

I used it to add excitement to my life—to face the challenge of being pregnant at 13 and to be told he'd deny it. For the good of the family, of course. (It was a false alarm, I was not pregnant.)

I used it as an excuse to marry an alcoholic at 19. It was a challenge to see if I could endure 13 more years of misery.

I used it to make myself cry. I just love to cry and feel sorry for myself. Swollen eyes are so attractive on me.

And wow, has it ever come in handy as a topic for therapy. I'll bet I can get years more mileage out of this without even trying.

And I'm not done "using" this yet. I love to be angry. I love pain and conflict. I love feeling like a piece of shit who's worth nothing.

I spent my whole life worrying about what would happen if I told my mother. Well, now I know what will happen; nothing, nothing, nothing. I'm worth nothing.[3] ❖

## Lee

### *"Mary of Nazareth"*

Mary of Nazareth was frightened. She felt surrounded by evil. A demon inhabited her father, and Mary was afraid that there was a demon in her too. She felt so strange sometimes, trembling and crying, and her dreams were full of terrifying images. Ever since her mother had died, the demons had been pursuing her. One came at night into her bed in the form of her father. Mary wasn't sure sometimes if she was awake or in a nightmare.

Mary had so much work to do, yet she was tired and sick all the time. Mary was beginning to suspect that she was with child. This possibility filled her with panic and despair. She was engaged to Joseph, but he would reject her when he discovered her pregnancy. Furthermore, the child of a demon would be a monster.

Death seemed the only answer. Dragging herself to the river in the middle of the night, Mary collapsed, sobbing in despair. She was so ashamed and so full of fear, but she didn't want to die. She prayed to Jehovah and even to the tree and river spirits. She begged the demons to leave her in peace. Exhausted, she just lay there by the river.

The noise of water over the rocks was soothing. Mary watched the early morning mist rise. It seemed as if she could see a figure in the mist. After a while she thought she heard a voice from the mist; she wasn't sure. It was her mother's voice she thought. The misty voice spoke; "Mary, don't be afraid, babies are a gift from God, and you are blessed. This is a very special baby. God loves you and the baby very much. Be at peace, all will be well."

Mary felt comforted. She closed her eyes. "Jesus," she thought, "I will name the baby Jesus, gift of God. I will go from this place and my demon father and visit my Aunt Elisabeth, she will help me."

Mary went to Elisabeth in a far-off village. Elisabeth was full of joy to see her niece. "I have such news for you, Mary, but you probably have guessed from looking at me! A baby, after 20 years of marriage to dear Zacharias, we are having a baby! It's a miracle!"

Mary just fell at her aunt's feet, weeping and fatigued. "Oh, Aunt, I am so happy for you!" Nevertheless, Mary continued to sob hysterically. "I am having a baby too, but Joseph is not the father. I don't know what to do!"

Elisabeth was calm but troubled at Mary's news. "It was your father, wasn't it?" she asked. Mary just nodded, wordless.

"I was afraid of that when my sister died. He is a weak man. I tried to convince him to send you to me, but he insisted on keeping you with him to run the household." She sighed,

"Mary dear, you stay with me. I'll speak to your father and Joseph. Don't worry, when I'm done with them, they won't dare peep."

Mary said, "Before I came here, I had a vision from mother. She said that everything would be okay, that babies are from God.

"Indeed they are!" Elisabeth replied with vigor. "The villagers are already whispering that my baby must be a miracle from God because I am so old. We'll tell them that your baby is also a miracle, a blessing from God."

So Elisabeth and Mary had their miracle babies and taught us that all babies are miracles of life and love. Both women were wise mothers and raised wise and extraordinary sons who became strong, brave prophets and teachers.[4] ❖

## Terri

### *"To My Brother"*

You molested me. There is a sense of freedom just in writing the words. The secret is out in the open for all to see and you are to blame, not me! So many things made sense to me after I remembered. The majority of the problems I've had in my relationship with my husband are the direct result of the abuse. I have never allowed myself to fully trust him because you taught me only too well that those I trust will betray and hurt me. I also assumed, incorrectly, the responsibility and guilt for what you did.

I thought I must have done something wrong. I thought I must surely be unlovable and unworthy of any kind of healthy affection.

I want to set the record straight. I was in no way responsible! I was an innocent child who was starved for affection and acceptance. You took advantage of my needs and used me to fulfill your own desires. You should have loved me and protected me as a brother to a sister. Instead, you molested me. Even if I didn't fight you and went along with what you wanted, you were and still are responsible. I tried to pass it off as "normal curiosity." There was nothing "normal" about it. You're six years older than me and you were certainly old enough to know better at the time.

I don't know what kind of relationship we can have now, or even what kind of contact I want with you. There is one thing I know for certain. There can be no relationship at all if you do not assume responsibility for what you did to me. I do not want to hear from you that you've "given it all up to the Lord" or that you've "asked God for forgiveness." You didn't molest God or destroy part of His life. You molested me and destroyed my innocence, and if you want forgiveness for what you did, you need to ask it of me!

I cannot stress enough how horribly this has affected my life: The nights I've stayed awake for hours thinking about it. The times when the pain was so great I could scarcely breathe. The months I couldn't make love with my husband for fear of seeing your face. This is what you've done to me. I just want you to know.[5] ❖

## A Program for Prophetic Ministry: Introduction

The following program for "Prophetic Ministry" addresses what is perhaps one of our nation's most difficult social issues: the sexual abuse of our children. Throughout the long history of denial, the pain and the reality has remained in the hearts of the children. The voices of the child victims and the millions of adult survivors have been silenced, not by violence, but by a deaf ear. It is a difficult subject to hear about, to believe. But since the sexual abuse of our children touches every corner of our society, *hearing* about it is the first and necessary step toward healing and social change.

Many people merely hear the statistics and cringe. 1 in every 4 girls and 1 in every 6 boys has been or will be sexually abused before reaching the age of 18. This means that approximately 20% of our population is personally affected by child sexual abuse. The realization of this fact has changed the way I view the world; it has changed the way I look at any group of people. One in every five people—young and old, rich and poor, male and female, black and white, Christian and Jew—carry the secret scars of child sexual abuse. With this vision, I "see" the people in the line at the grocery store, the congregation gathered in church, the students in classes, the commuters on the bus, my colleagues, my family, my friends. The sexual abuse of children touches all of our lives.

In order for individual and societal healing to happen, we need to hear and believe the silent cries as well as the horrible details of abuse that this 20% of our population needs to speak. Don't imagine that this hearing will be easy. It won't be. The listener often becomes too distressed to hear, and so we listeners need to practice. We need to build up our tolerance for hearing and embracing unbelievable horror. Victims and survivors of child sexual abuse need to feel heard and accepted, even though their experience of the world and their behaviors don't exactly make sense to us. Under the circumstances of their lives, their experiences and behaviors make perfect sense—*if only we would listen.* What is most important for us to remember is that behind the sterile, distancing statistics are graphically abusive experiences, many even more horrifying than the ones chosen for this book. Experiences that are too horrifying to even imagine; experiences that are heartbreaking, infuriating, sickening, totally unbelievable. But these experiences are tightly woven into the fabric of the lives of the victims, and they will never be able to shed those garments completely.

If it is difficult for us to hear about the realities and the specifics of child sexual abuse, just try to imagine how difficult it is for those who must live—every day and every night—with the abuse and the after-effects of the abuse.

Religious communities have the power and the opportunity to come to the aid of the victims, and to begin shifting the collective consciousness. As outlined in the previous chapter, some denominations have already begun to work toward this goal. Being aware of existing programs and ideas, and incorporating them into the new programs will enhance both the existing and the new.

The proposed program for "Prophetic Ministry" on child sexual abuse offers a different way to approach the subject. Returning to the focus of "hearing," the program stresses EDUCATION. I am convinced that raising the collective consciousness of religious Americans about the issue of child sexual abuse is essential and primary to healing and change. However, rather than educating the powerless child victims, which is currently the most widely-accepted type of prevention effort, those with power [church leaders, clergy, religious educators, adults] are the focus of education.

The educational goal of PHASE ONE of the proposed "Prophetic Ministry" Program is "desensitization." In the early 1980s, the Boston-area Women in Crisis Committee of the Episcopal Church refused a grant request from an agency offering support and therapy to female survivors of incest. Members of the Committee were reluctant and squeamish about the grant; one member actually said, "Incest is just too sleazy."[6] There is no question that the sexual abuse of children is a topic which is sleazy beyond description. It is, however, a topic we all need to hear about and learn about so our children can be protected from experiences which some intelligent, caring adults consider too sleazy to discuss. Desensitization to the issue does not mean moving toward an emotional hardening of heart, but toward a softened level of tolerance that will allow people to hear the truth and the pain; tolerance that will allow people to create a place in their hearts which can welcome and embrace the victims with compassion. The softening of hearts and the changing of attitudes will not happen quickly or easily. Therefore, the steps toward the goal must be constant and relentless. 5000 years of blindness and deafness has built a thick, high wall of denial that can only be dismantled with care and safety; but that dismantling truly needs to begin today.

Thankfully, the Women in Crisis Committee of the Episcopal Church in Boston has since become educated and desensitized; they currently publish impressive materials on the subject of child sexual abuse, offer support to victims and survivors, and award grant money to agencies working with survivors.

Child sexual abuse as a JUSTICE issue within religious communities requires and deserves attention separate from both family/domestic violence programs and child advocacy programs. The existence of child sexual abuse and the seriousness of this moral crime have been ignored and denied forever. By including child sexual abuse with other issues, further denial is invited. In most hearts and minds, the issue remains so sleazy that any opportunity for avoidance will be appreciated and taken—consciously or unconsciously. Yet by acknowledging and including child sexual abuse with other programs, religious communities might be lulled into believing that the issue has, in fact, been addressed . . . while still, the plague rages on and the souls of millions perish.

Domestic violence has recently become the more generic, less specific term for "wife-battering." Including child sexual abuse with domestic violence mistakenly implies that it is a women's issue. The power dynamic of child sexual abuse is, however, vastly different from the power dynamic of wife-battering. Often physical violence is not involved; and never can the relationship between the child and the adult perpetrator be considered an equal partnership. In further support of the mistaken implication that child sexual abuse is a women's issue is the reality that most justice programs focusing on child sexual abuse are sponsored by women in ministry departments. *But child sexual abuse is not just a women's issue.* Current estimates indicate that one in every six boys is sexually abused before reaching the age of 18, and that 85% of the perpetrators of child sexual abuse are male.[7] Child sexual abuse is very much a men's issue, too.

Child Advocacy programs also tend to evade child sexual abuse by focusing on the issues which are often a bit more removed from the experiences of our own communities than is child sexual abuse. These efforts are often directed toward foreign countries.[8]

Child sexual abuse adversely affects all of society, not just children. Viewing it as a child-specific issue forgets the millions of adult survivors who also need attention from their religious communities.

The "Prophetic Ministry" Program suggests ways to develop a basic, consciousness-raising program for adults, and focuses on achieving widespread, attitudinal change. Admittedly, this is a program with long-range goals and it will require commitment, patience and persistence. Some people who are truly committed to working on this issue might become discouraged by not seeing concrete results within a short period of time. Therefore, other ideas for intervention, prevention, and pastoral care and counseling activities, which can be implemented more quickly, have been included throughout the program. This program is intended not as a "gospel," but as a sample. Its goal is to plant seeds and light sparks within the committed hearts and creative minds of each religious individual and each religious community. *Any* words spoken about the issue of child sexual abuse, *any* actions taken will only help in the healing. There is no right or wrong way to begin. The most important key is to say something; do something!

Another important key to a successful program and to healing was stressed by the name change of the "Safe Kids Program" to "Community Sexual Abuse Prevention Program." This key is well within the reach and the power of the religious communities. *Name* the "Prophetic Ministry" program appropriately: *Child Sexual Abuse: A Moral Emergency!*

## Phases of a Prophetic Ministry Program

## PHASE ONE

*A. Education of Religious Leaders: Clergy, Seminarians, Officials*

*B. Consciousness Raising for Adults*

A.  EDUCATION OF RELIGIOUS LEADERS: An on-going effort to educate clergy and seminarians about the issue of child sexual abuse is an urgent need. Rather than relying on pastoral counseling classes at seminaries to "touch" upon the issue, it is recommended that the credentialing bodies within religious institutions require mandatory attendance at conferences, workshops and trainings on the subject of child sexual abuse. These trainings need not have a religious focus. Any type of professional, interdisciplinary information will be helpful. Mandatory attendance is strongly advised because, as demonstrated by historical and current denial, child sexual abuse as an issue for attention, study and involvement will be avoided as long as possible.

It is more difficult to mandate training for previously-ordained clergy and religious leaders than for seminarians, although it certainly is not impossible to accomplish. However, in lieu of mandated training, it is recommended that those currently in power within the religious organizations demonstrate the importance of education through their own attention, interest and actions around the issue, thus encouraging others to become informed.

It is recommended that education for clergy, seminarians, and religious leaders and officials begin slowly, so as not to overwhelm and alienate them, but by all means, comprehensively. Introductory presentation topics for this population could include history, statistics, impact, offender profile, pastoral response, laws, and myths.

A possible, although not predictable, result of even introductory education is the recovery of buried memories of child sexual abuse. Therefore, it is a good idea to be prepared to offer support groups or counseling referrals for religious leaders who have been sexually abused as children. Dealing with their own victimization will then allow these religious leaders to be more attentive and responsive to victims and survivors. This personal work should be encouraged since denial is actually rooted in repressed memories of victimization and/or offending.

B. CONSCIOUSNESS-RAISING FOR ADULTS: In order to even hope that the issue of child sexual abuse will be considered as a serious social problem by members of religious communities, it is important that the subject be repeatedly mentioned from the pulpit. Victims and survivors need to hear and believe that their religious community is a safe place. Perpetrators of child sexual abuse need to hear that the sexual abuse of children is not only morally wrong and destructive, but a serious crime as well. Pastors, rabbis, and other religious leaders who have already preached on the subject deserve recognition and appreciation for their courage and commitment. However, just one sermon in 1000 or 2000 different religious communities during one year will not even begin to dent the wall of denial protecting this 5000-year-old systemic problem. Furthermore, there may be a tendency to believe that with one sermon, the issue has been sufficiently addressed. A sermon on the subject of child sexual abuse is an excellent beginning; but clearly there is much more work to be done.

Toward consciousness-raising, a sermon series consisting of six sermons, with one delivered every other month for one year, is proposed in PHASE ONE as the primary method of educating adults. Within religious communities, this raising of consciousness and the changing of attitudes can begin, effectively, simply by asking people, at first, to do nothing more than listen and hear about the issue of child sexual abuse. Examples of how a religious sermon can focus directly and sensitively on the emergency of child sexual abuse are included, as reference, in Appendix 5. Each sermon reflects the different ways of knowing and the different life experiences of its author, as well as meeting the needs of the hearers of a particular religious perspective.

After one sermon, some people [usually survivors] may feel motivated to "do something," but this level of interest is doubtful and not to be expected. If a religious leader is approached by an interested member of the community who wants to take action toward preventing child sexual abuse during PHASE ONE, the religious leader can be prepared with a bibliography [or preferably a lending library] of suggested reading, and videos for viewing. These resources could offer some ideas for appropriate action within the community. These action-oriented members could be invited to participate in future services, to begin gathering resources [books, films, and/or speakers for PHASE TWO], or to begin an outreach into the community, offering church facilities [at no charge] to community agencies and groups which support victims and survivors, and/or provide education specific to child sexual abuse.

As a specific intervention effort, action-oriented members could initiate contact with the appropriate offices within the religious institution and/or state government in order to begin gathering the resources needed to develop specific procedures for reporting suspected abuse from within religious communities.

As a specific prevention effort, action-oriented members might choose to implement an education program for the children which would coincide with and complement the sermon series for adults. Several religious organizations already have excellent curricula for children, as do any number of state agencies. These prevention programs geared for children are therefore readily and easily accessible.

## PHASE TWO

*A. Repeat Phase One: Education of Religious Leaders and Consciousness-raising of Adults*

*B. Lecture/discussion Series*

A.  REPEAT PHASE ONE: *Education of Religious Leaders*: It is suggested that the education of religious leaders be an ongoing and continuous effort.   There is so much to learn, so much to hear, that this effort could easily continue—requiring one or two trainings a year on the topics already mentioned (history, statistics, impact, offenders, pastoral response, laws, and myths)—for several years without becoming repetitive.

*Consciousness-raising of Adults:* The PHASE ONE sermon series, or additional sermons, may need to be repeated for several years before any interest in action from within the community spontaneously arises.  But don't be discouraged; the community is still trying to hear.  It is imperative that the "invitation to hear" continues to be extended.  Adding a sermon discussion immediately following each sermon on child sexual abuse might be helpful to the community.  Inviting people to hear AND talk often stirs up an interest in action.

B. LECTURE/DISCUSSION SERIES: During PHASE TWO, it is suggested that a quarterly lecture/discussion series be added to the program.  There are large numbers of professionals and experts [survivors can be considered "experts"] currently working in the field of child sexual abuse all across the country, perhaps already established in every religious community.  These professionals and experts can be invited to volunteer as guest speakers on any variety of topics related to child sexual abuse.  Numerous educational videos as well as privately-produced Hollywood films are available to supplement the lecture/discussion series.

The sermons and lectures need not all be delivered by the pastor or rabbi or specific religious leader of the community; however, in order for people in the community to believe that child sexual abuse is truly a serious issue, the presence and the involvement of the religious leader in every sermon, discussion and lecture will underscore the importance of the issue in the eyes of God and the hearts of humans.

At any time during PHASES ONE and TWO, the religious leader(s) need to be prepared to hear and receive disclosures of sexual abuse from both victims and perpetrators. This will be an especially challenging part of the program. Previous training on handling these situations is strongly advised. However, a particularly good resource has been published by the Women in Crisis Committee of the Episcopal Diocese of Massachusetts. *Responding to Incest: In Memory of Nancy* was produced by the Episcopal Church specifically for religious leaders and is designed as an aid for responding to the disclosure of victims and survivors. Other denominations are encouraged, at least, to provide this or a similar reference to religious leaders. Specific training is preferable.

## PHASE THREE

A. *Repeat Phases One and Two: Education/Consciousness-raising*
*Lecture/Discussion*

B. *Political Action*

C. *Community Outreach*

D. *Inter-religious and Denominational Conferences*

E. *Parish-sponsored Counseling Groups for Victims and Survivors*

A. REPEAT PHASE ONE AND TWO: PHASE THREE may naturally evolve at any time during PHASE ONE or PHASE TWO, and this natural evolution needs to be welcomed and supported *whenever it arises*; however, it's not necessary to "rush" into PHASE THREE. Instead, patiently repeat PHASES ONE and TWO until an interest in the suggested PHASE THREE activities—or other creative suggestions from community members—evolves, spontaneously, from within the community. But, if an interest in action doesn't evolve for a long, long time, don't be discouraged; and most importantly, don't consider abandoning the program from this seeming lack of interest; the truth is being spoken, and some *are* hearing it; seeds are being sown; attitudes are silently shifting. God's work is being done.

B. POLITICAL ACTION: It is important for religious leaders to become aware of the political and legislative issues surrounding child sexual abuse which currently exist in their own states; these regulations vary widely. State legislators and district attorneys can provide a wealth of information, as can state and local child protective service agencies. Members of the community are encouraged to research the laws and decide which changes in legislation they would like to support. They, in turn, can invite the rest of the community to participate in lobbying, petition signing, letter-writing campaigns, etc. State legislators, district attorneys, AND representatives from agencies could be especially helpful and eager guest speakers during PHASE TWO.

C. COMMUNITY OUTREACH: Outreach in the community, beyond the wall of the religious community, offers broad opportunities for action by members. Involvement with schools, parent groups, YM/YWCAs, youth organizations, Boys and Girls clubs, Big Brother and Big Sister organizations, counseling agencies and local companies can begin by inviting these organizations to lectures and discussions, or by offering to provide a workshop/lecture/discussion for them. Creativity in this area is encouraged! Getting the information about child sexual abuse and the religious organization's serious commitment to stopping it out into the community is the desired goal.

D. INTER-RELIGIOUS AND DENOMINATIONAL CONFERENCES: Sponsoring, supporting, and initiating conferences and workshops for all populations is encouraged. Especially interesting would be conferences combining "state" and religion. Involve local law enforcement agencies and district attorney's offices, especially when there is an interest in reporting laws and procedures. Since child sexual abuse is a moral and a legal issue, religious communities can inform the justice system, and the justice system can inform the religious communities. Just like the prosecutor and the ethicist!

It is recommended that any outreach into the wider community, including the offering of conferences, begin slowly.

Too much information—or information that is too horrifying—will serve only to add more and thicker stone to the wall of denial. Too much and/or too horrible cannot be tolerated. So, go slowly but steadily, patiently but persistently. It is important that a solid foundation be carefully laid before asking people to move onto the next level of awareness or to take on the next activity.

E. COUNSELING GROUPS: Many religious communities have a budget for social concerns programs, and some ministers manage a sizeable discretionary fund. A 12-week psychotherapy group for either child victims or adult survivors could be completely financed for approximately $1200 - $2400.[9] Members of the church could interview and hire a therapist, provide space, and then reach out into the community and invite victims or survivors to participate for no cost.

Group therapy is a supportive and effective, albeit costly method of healing, and is strongly recommended for victims and survivors of child sexual abuse. Unfortunately, many survivors cannot afford *any* type of therapy. A church-sponsored counseling program is the most important pastoral response a congregation can have to the realities of child sexual abuse. This program could literally save a life!

# CHAPTER SEVEN

# *God Works in Mysterious Ways: Hope for Healing and Change*

Each person is responsible to God and to History for what he or she did or did not do.
— Duane Draper, AIDS Action Committee, Boston

## Eve

### *"The Flip-Sides of 'Why Me, God?'"*

SIDE ONE:

Why me, God?
Why was I ever born?
Why was I the one chosen to be sacrificed to these parents?
Why did you let my Dad rape me?  And my Mom, where was
    she?
Why didn't Mom help me?

Why did I have to suffer so then, and still?
    I tried to be such a good girl.
Why didn't they love me?
    Oh, how I loved them.
Why did I have to be sick and frightened all the time?
Why didn't I ever feel safe enough to sleep or laugh . . . or cry?

Why did I waste so much of my life hating myself?
Why did I try to fill the void with so many penises?
    Each one stretching the emptiness until it swallowed me.
    Sobbing.
Why did I, do I, have so many tears to cry?
Why did I have to endure such shameful abuse from family,

friends and lovers?
I just wanted someone—needed someone—to love me.

Oh, God.  Why didn't they love me?
Why was I lost in hell, all alone, for most of my life?
    And it was hell, the not-knowing, the trying to run away
    from myself with pills and alcohol and sex and lies.
Why didn't it work?
Why couldn't I run away from me?
    I wanted to.  I wanted to die.


SIDE TWO:

Why me, God?
Why didn't I completely lose myself?
    I tried, but I just couldn't abandon me.
Why didn't I die in a car accident on one of those many nights
    I was too drunk to even see, too drunk to even remember
    driving home?
Why did I keep searching so relentlessly for the roots of my
    sorrow and my desire to destroy myself?
Why didn't my dreams of suicide and my longing for death
    ever materialize into reality?

God, Why am I not still longing for death?
Why did I move onto a healthier, happier time?
Why did I stop trying to get away from me?
Why—and when—did I start to love me?
    I've met survivors with multiple-personality disorder.
Why am I still only "just one" me?
    And the survivor who was paranoid brought her terror into
    my life and my home.  Nothing else has ever frightened me
    so much.
Why her and not me?

    My cousin, also abused, is psychotic and totally lost to this
    world.
Why me, God?  Why am I not psychotic?
Why was I chosen to break through the denial and to begin
    healing?
Why did I choose such wonderful doctors, ones who could
    tolerate my truth, ones who didn't encourage me to block it

out with drugs, ones who were there and who helped me to pick up the pieces when my whole life crumbled?

Why did I have the strength to tolerate and deal with all of this pain?
Pain I thought was terminal. Pain which could've been terminal if I had acted on any one of my many plans to end it.

I've lived the consequences of incest, and my life has been hell.
But every time I see the psychotic woman who screams at the invisible people on the streets in my neighborhood,
Every time I see the glassy stare of my once-brilliant friend who is now 23 separate personalities,
Every time I think of my cousin's lost soul,
Every time I hear of the multitudes of people who are controlled by addictions to food or drugs or sex,
Every time I hear that someone who was molested as a child grew up and became a child molester,
Every time I see and hear how devastating the consequences of incest can be,
I feel grateful because I know that given the circumstances of my childhood, my life—my hell on earth—could have been much, much worse.

Why me, God?
Why was I spared from having to live through an even worse nightmare?[1] ❖

## Linda

### *"A Life-changing Moment"*

Every time a television talk show discussed the issue of child sexual abuse, I felt a suffocating pressure inside me. Abused by my father at a very young age, I had spent most of my adult life trying to avoid the issue. Trying to forget the evenings when my mother would be away and I would hear the creak on the stairs. At an early age, I learned to "tune out" the horror and the disgust, but NOT the shame.

My adult life has been best characterized as a five-ring circus, where I have been wife, mom, career-woman, faithful church worker, and loving daughter. Bouts with depression were eased by medication, but that was like putting a band-aid on the deep gash in my soul.

Two years ago, when my perfect world was threatened by financial ruin, I knew that it was time for professional help. My faith in God had always been strong, but I thought it, too, had failed me. Therapy showed me the way to explore the depths of my pain, and to learn to deal with it. Coincidentally, the adult Bible study at my church began a course on understanding the spiritual disciplines. While healing my mind through therapy, God was healing my soul by showing me that I was the one who had broken the connection—God had always been there.

The final turning point in my healing, that life-changing moment, came at the 1992 Annual Meeting of the Massachusetts Conference of the United Church of Christ. One of the resolutions to be voted on was "Breaking the Silence and Ending the Cycle of Child Sexual Abuse." When this resolution was proposed, the familiar heavy feeling descended on me. "I am NOT going to speak," I told myself. "It won't be necessary—who would speak against this resolution?" Then someone presented an amendment that would have deleted the words, "children at risk of abuse." Suddenly I knew that I couldn't keep silent. Something, or Someone, pushed me from my seat to the microphone. I hate speaking extemporaneously, yet the words came clearly to me, "My name is Linda—and I AM a victim of childhood sexual abuse. Because I have kept silent, two generations of children have been put at risk; my daughters, my nieces, and my granddaughters. Tomorrow I plan to go to my parents' house to break that cycle because I fear a neighbor's child even now may be at risk." The outpouring of support and caring from delegates and friends that afternoon sustained me through the pain and denial that was to come when I confronted my parents the next day.

After several months, my father is now speaking to me again. However, there has been no acknowledgment by him of the abuse. My mother, after all these years, doesn't feel that she can live any differently—mostly for socioeconomic reasons, she says.

And so it would seem that nothing much has changed, yet the disclosure has made the world of difference to me. I know that the pain of my childhood can be used to help others. This fall I entered college, and with God's help have begun the long journey to ordained ministry.

God truly works in mysterious ways![2] ❖

## Hope for Healing: Change

Why do adults sexually abuse children? This is the question I am most often asked. And it is THE most difficult question to answer, particularly from a religious perspective. There appears to be no reasonable answer; however, some psychological theories do attempt to provide an explanation in lieu of a reasonable answer:

- People who sexually abuse children are often repeating what they experienced in childhood. Although not all victims of child sexual abuse grow up to be molesters of other children, a high percentage of convicted child molesters—this is the only population of molesters available to be surveyed—do report having been abused in childhood.

- The sexual abuse of children by adults and older children is about power. Sex becomes the method by which the need to feel powerful is acted out. Often child molesters are anti-social, or have difficulty maintaining satisfying adult relationships. Often they feel inadequate with their peers. With helpless children, molesters feel powerful, in control, and accepted. It is difficult for children to effectively say no and thus "reject" their abusers.

- The sexual abuse of children can be a compulsion or even an addiction. The abuser is out of control. The actual sexual experiences ease tension . . . feel good . . . good enough to help the abuser regain control . . . until the next urge, the next time.

People with a religious orientation often press the questioning further, beyond the psychological explanations. Where is God? Where is God in this situation which clearly is immoral and inevitably leads to the destruction of innocent souls? How can God let this happen? Why?

I've heard some religious leaders answer these questions with what they explain as *"faith."* "It happens for *a reason.*" And I respond, "What reason? What possible reason?"

There is nothing within "reason" about any aspect of the sexual abuse of children. There is nothing reasonable about the act and nothing reasonable about the explanations for why it happens. This religious explanation of "faith" sounds too much like denial creeping back into the discussion. It sounds like a desperate attempt to make sense of total absurdity. It sounds like an excuse for acceptance and passivity.

Many survivors have found meaning through their own healing processes, meaning through helping other victims and survivors, yet still, there is no *"reason"* for this abuse. There is no grand, cosmic scheme. The abuse is not "God's will." There is no reason for millions of innocent souls to suffer and perish. No earthly reason. No heavenly reason. The sexual abuse of children is not an epidemic that needs to be made sense out of. It is an epidemic that needs to be stopped.

So, if not to be found in some mysterious reason yet to be revealed, then just where is God?

Many child victims and adult survivors turn to God, asking for interventions, asking for the abuse to stop. However, their requests of God are in vain, because God can't make the abuse stop. Human beings are given the gift of free will. Some choose to sexually abuse children. Others can choose to stop them.

But, still, the children turn to God for assistance; and when their prayers go unanswered, they feel abandoned by God, and become even more desperate. But perhaps God does, indeed, hear the silent cries of the children and responds to them through us. So now the victims and the survivors can turn to us and be heard and comforted.

So where—exactly—is God?

Perhaps God is in the concerned and committed religious leaders, doctors, lawyers, teachers, police officers, judges, counselors, and other helping professionals who aren't afraid to hear and speak the truth about child sexual abuse. Perhaps God is in the law-makers who seek justice and protection for the children.

Perhaps God is in the hearts of the courageous survivors who struggle to overcome one of life's greatest obstacles—the betrayal of their innocence—who struggle just to live.

Perhaps God is in the faces of the children. Perhaps God is that beam of light which shines through their eyes and into our hearts. So trusting, so loyal, searching only for our nurturing love.

Perhaps God is in the mind's ability to deny, the psyche's ability to repress, and the body's ability to dissociate. Perhaps these abilities are God's gifts to the victims and survivors of child sexual abuse so they can continue living. For surely, if they could not deny, repress, and dissociate, many children would die or go insane instantly at the moment of the abuse. And many more would take their own lives, desperate to end the pain.

Perhaps God is in the eternal Hope for healing.

Perhaps God is in the Spark which initiates and sustains the healing force.

Perhaps God is in every Voice which speaks.

Perhaps God is in every challenge to Act. "Through the prosecution of perpetrators of child sexual abuse who were, themselves, victims, we are punishing what we failed to prevent. Punitive sanction at the end of the line should not be our only approach to protecting children. Nothing we can do is more important than trying to prevent, TODAY, the terrible tragedies these children have to endure. We have the ability to make a difference. We know what to do. But do we have the will?"[3]

Perhaps God is in every ear which hears.

# APPENDIX 1

# *Definitions*

---

1.1.    Types of **Child Abuse**: Please note that the definition of "child" varies from state to state, as do the "age of consent" and the definitions of "abuse."

**Emotional Abuse** includes verbal abuse [i.e., name-calling, swearing, yelling], destruction of a healthy self-image, locking a child in a closed place, parentifying a child, etc. Emotional abuse is the most difficult type of child abuse to define and identify; it is, therefore, extremely damaging because it often remains undetected and untreated.

**Neglect** ranges from failing to provide adequate food to lack of cleanliness, to infant drug addiction, to actual death caused by lack of parental/caretaker attention.

**Physical Abuse** ranges from hitting to murder. With the exception of the extremely damaging situations, cases of physical abuse are often difficult to identify within any standard guidelines. Who draws the line between discipline and abuse? And where is the line drawn?

**Sexual Abuse** includes forcible rape of a child, rape of a child, assault with intent to rape a child, incest, indecent assault and battery, exploitation, and indecent exposure.[1]

1.2.    The term **"Survivor"** has become a generic term usually applied to people, generally adults, who are not currently being victimized. The term does not reflect any particular state of well-being. Consistent with Webster's definition, a survivor is one who continues to "live or exist" after the sexual abuse has stopped. There are no distinctions made, however, regarding the quality of life following the abuse. In order to be considered a survivor of child sexual abuse, one simply needs to still be alive.

The survivor continuum of life-experiences is vast and varied. The possible reactions following child sexual abuse range from successful suicide attempts to healthy adult functioning. Along the continuum, some survivors' lives include the experiences of multiple personality disorder, violence, depression, substance abuse, prostitution, abusive relationships, workaholism, professional success at the expense of personal relationships.

1.3. Sexual **"Violence"** Against Children: Any sexual interaction with children is considered violence because of its criminal nature, even if physical force is not used. The violation of a child's body is violent because it is done without the child's consent, and often with the child in fear. One of the definitions of "violent" offered by Webster includes the state of being excited to the point of "loss of control." An adult who has any kind of sexual involvement with a child has definitely lost control.

1.4. In recent years, the word **"Incest"** has sometimes been inaccurately used as the all-encompassing description for any type of child sexual abuse by any perpetrator, regardless of the relationship to the child. By its basic definition, incest describes sexual interactions between people who are related; age is not necessarily a factor. Incest is not specific to adult sexual interactions with children, but to the nature of the blood relationships of the people involved.

Some authors, professionals, and survivors use the word incest carefully, maintaining the integrity of its definition; others do not.

1.5 Literally, **"Disclose"** means to open up, to expose to view, or to make known something previously held as secret. Although "disclosure" has become the clinical word for "telling" about child sexual abuse, the literal definition helps us to understand that when victims and survivors disclose, they do much more then merely "tell"; they "open," "expose," "reveal" themselves, and are thus, extremely vulnerable.

# APPENDIX 2

# *Statistics*

2.1. It is difficult to document the number of children who are sexually abused each year in the United States. "The Resource Packet for Religious Leaders," published by the National Committee for Prevention of Child Abuse, indicates that "Nationwide, over 2 million children are reported per year as suspected victims of child abuse and neglect." This number represents all forms of child abuse: emotional, physical and sexual, as well as neglect. 1300 children die from their injuries; 100,000 were victims of sexual abuse in 1984; 80,000 cases of emotional maltreatment were reported in 1986. [2]

The information is difficult to compile and tabulate because social service agencies in the 50 United States have diverse methods of reporting, as well as different laws and different legal definitions of "child" and "abuse."

In 1986, the American Humane Association collected data on child sexual abuse; according to their information, 140,000 reports are filed each year.[3] Also in 1986, Westat, Inc. conducted the "Second National Incidence Study of Child Abuse and Neglect." The revised estimate of their findings indicate that 133,600 children are sexually abused each year.[4] "The federal government ended its contract with the American Association for the Protection of Children, which had collected national child abuse statistics since 1976, so that no statistics will be available for 1988 or 1989. A new data collection system was supposed to be in place to collect and publish statistics for 1990 and beyond, but many observers believe that the earliest possible statistics will be for 1991 or maybe even 1992."[5]

118

According to researchers at The National Resource Center on Child Sexual Abuse, this data is not yet available in 1992. An effort is being made to standardize state reporting procedures so accurate statistics will be available in the near future.

**2.2** Some "Actual Statistics" are available from State and county sources:

# CALIFORNIA

STATE DATA:

1991 state data on Child Abuse was compiled by the Department of Social Services, Statistical Services Branch, and provided by the California Consortium for the Prevention of Child Abuse, Sacremento, CA, with the following explanation: "This is an unduplicated count of those children reported as abused or neglected *and* whose cases reached Child Protective Services Emergency Response disposition during 1991. Because of recent reductions in state funding for child welfare services, standards for initiating emergency response have been raised, and consequently an increased number of reports are identified as not warranting emergency response. These screened out reports are not reflected in these tabulations."

### 1991 Child Abuse Reports in California

| TYPE | NUMBER | PERCENT |
|---|---|---|
| Neglect | 204,299 | 36% |
| Physical Abuse | 184,681 | 32% |
| Sexual Abuse | 102,200 | 18% |
| Caretaker Absence/ | | |
| Incapacity | 55,351 | 10% |
| Emotional Abuse | 22,586 | 4% |
| Child Exploitation | 2,097 | |
| Total | 571,214 | |

SAN DIEGO COUNTY DATA:
Reporting statistics were compiled by the Child Abuse Unit of the San Diego County Sheriff's Department for the fiscal years of 90/91 and 91/92 and provided by Detective Dana Gassaway.
Excludes the City of San Diego
Jurisdiction Population: 705,278

*Reported Cases of Child Molestation:*
FY 90/91 - 1644
FY 91/92 - 1671

*Child Molestations Cases Assigned for Investigation:*
FY 90/91 - 742
FY 91/92 - 666
[Of the 1,103 total child abuse cases assigned for criminal investigation FY 91/92, 61% were child sexual molestation, 28% were physical child abuse, and 11% were child neglect.]

# MASSACHUSETTS

STATE DATA:
1991 Child Abuse Reports were compiled by The Department of Social Services (DSS) and provided by The Children's Trust Fund.
*Child Abuse Reports received by DSS - 1991*
Total:                              88,748

Investigated and
Confirmed:                          28,048

Referred to District
Attorney:                            2,858

MIDDLESEX COUNTY DATA:
Population: 1,398,468
Mainly Urban and Suburban
Number of child sexual abuse cases referred to the District Attorney in 1991: 711

HAMPSHIRE/FRANKLIN COUNTIES DATA:
Population: 216,660
Small urban centers and rural communities:
Number of child sexual abuse cases referred to the District
Attorney in 1991: 317

In February, 1992, I attempted to gather the actual number of child sexual abuse cases referred to the 11 District Attorney's Offices in Massachusetts because the Middlesex County DA was planning to give a speech on child sexual abuse to a state-wide audience. I called the other 10 offices, identifying myself as working at the Middlesex Child Unit, gathering data for the previously-noted reason. Four of the 10 offices responded immediately by sending me detailed reports. One office had just switched to a new computer system and said they would send stats ASAP, but never did. One office called and left a message for me with just one number; 479 reports of child sexual abuse were referred to their office in 1991. Two offices never returned my call after several attempts. Two offices refused to provide me with the data.

Although I didn't receive the data I wanted, I did experience, first-hand, the frustration of trying to gather accurate statistics. If I could not successfully gather data from 10 district attorneys' offices from within one small state, even when I identified myself as working for the 11th district attorney, I can understand why national statistics are not available. Changes are desperately needed in the methods of compiling and gathering statistics regarding child sexual abuse.

# OHIO

CUYAHUGA COUNTY DATA:
The information was compiled by Child Welfare intake of the Ohio Department of Social Services and provided by The Community Sexual Abuse Prevention Program, Cleveland, OH.
Cuyahoga County includes Cleveland and northeast Ohio.

*Kids' Reports Assigned for Investigation*
January - September 1992:     1398
(Avg = 155/month)
October - December 1992
(estimated) 155 x 3:                    465

Total:                                         1863

# WASHINGTON

STATE DATA:
   State statistics were compiled by the Office of Child Protective Services and provided by Rick Winters.
   75,476 reports of child maltreatment, involving 62,000 children, were registered with child protective services in 1991. Obviously, this discrepancy in numbers indicates that some children experienced more than one type of maltreatment.
   14,338 reports involved child sexual abuse.

KING COUNTY DATA:
   Information was compiled and provided by the King County Sheriff's Office.
   Jurisdiction includes unincorporated King County and excludes Seattle.
   Population: 600,000.

*1991 Child Abuse Cases referred to the Sexual Assault Unit— King County Sheriff's Office:*

   Child Rape              142
   Child Molestation    444

   Total:                     586
   Physical Abuse        745

   The total number of sexual offenses (adult and children) referred to the Sheriff's office in 1991 was 2598. Child sexual abuse represents 23% of the total. An additional 745 cases of physical child abuse were referred to the King County Sheriff's Office.

# Comments

I found the "actual statistics" provided to me by these agencies both horrifying and fascinating. Certain state and county agencies and departments are doing an excellent job tracking and reporting the data regarding child sexual abuse. However, even in this brief presentation, the variations in gathering and reporting the data are painfully obvious. Some statistics represent "emergency" reports, some represent all reports, some represent "investigations," some represent referrals to district attorneys for prosecution. Some states require that all referrals of child abuse go through the department of social services, some states require that certain reports be handled by the department of social services and others by law enforcement agencies.

This information is all very interesting, but is it helpful to the growing number of concerned individuals who are trying to understand just how many children are being sexually victimized in America? And do the statistics accurately represent the actual abuse? Do the statistics really matter?

**2.3.** Child Sexual Abuse Offender: Prosecutions

According to Boston area therapist Linda T. Sanford, child molesters are rarely caught or punished in the United States. Sanford indicated that in order for a molester to actually be sentenced to prison, he/she has to make that particular goal a "mission" by being repetitive, or violent or by abusing a number of children.[6]

From July 1989 to December 1990, the Child Abuse Prosecution Unit of the Middlesex County District Attorney's Office received 1,051 reports of child abuse. [The specific type of abuse is not separated in this number, nor in the following prosecution dispositions.] 783 investigations were completed: 26.5% (208 cases) resulted in prosecutions; 73.4% (575 cases) were closed without prosecution.[7]

**2.4.** The Closed Investigation Report from the Middlesex County Child Abuse Prosecution Unit indicates the following reasons for "NO PROSECUTION:" Child incompetent to testify, Insufficient Disclosure/Evidence, Child unwilling to Testify, Family Unsupportive of Investigation/Prosecution, Victim moved from Jurisdiction, No Case Jurisdiction, Perpetrator Unknown, Resolved without Prosecution, Therapeutically Inappropriate, Beyond Statute of Limitations.

# APPENDIX 3

# *Historical Timeline (Condensed from Chapter Four)*

| | |
|---|---|
| 3000 BCE | Sumerian clay tablets included accounts of and protests against the use of children for sex. |
| 2000 BCE | The Code of Hammurabi included punishments for adult men who had intercourse with girls. |

Hebrew Bible
Genesis 19:30-36
Lot's daughters "conspire" to lay with him.

Leviticus 18:6-18
"None of you shall approach one near of kin to him to uncover nakedness."

2 Samuel 13:1-29
Tamar is raped by her brother.
"No, my brother, do not force me . . . and being stronger than she, he forced her."

Mosaic Law
Injunctions against the corruption of children were included. "The penalty for sodomy with children over nine was death by stoning. Copulation with younger children was not considered a sexual act, and was punishable by a whipping as a matter of public discipline."

5th Century BCE   Pederastic relationships were common in ancient Greece. "The archetype Lover/Beloved relationship was between a mature man at the height of his sexual power and need and a young, erotically-undeveloped boy just before puberty."

| | |
|---|---|
| 4th Century BCE | Plato proposed the idea that children should be raised "in common." Aristotle objected because "when men had sex with boys, they wouldn't know if they were their own sons." |
| 1st Century CE | The Romans made an effort to protect free-born children from sexual abuse and punished this act severely. Abandoned children or slave children were used freely for sex. |
| 4th Century CE | Saint Augustine offered an opinion about childhood: "Who would not shudder, if he were given the choice of eternal death or life again as a child? Who would not choose to die?" |
| 7th Century CE | [Ireland] Dymphna resisted her father, the king, who wanted to marry her. She was subsequently beheaded by him. In the 13th Century Dymphna was named the patron saint of the mentally ill. |
| 13th Century CE | Saint Thomas Aquinas wrote extensively on "Sex and the Law of Nature." He separated sexual sins into sins "according to Nature" and sins "against Nature." Less serious were acts such as rape or incest (with a member of the opposite sex) because they were considered physically complete. The sexual sins against Nature—masturbation, homosexuality and beastiality—carried a more serious penance. |
| 15th Century CE | [France] In a sermon, Jean Gerson warned the child to prevent others from "touching him or kissing him, and if he has failed to (prevent this), he must report this in every instance in confession." |
| 17th Century CE | [France] Heroard, the physician for King Henry IV, kept a diary and recorded the details of Louis XIII's childhood. During the prince's "first three years, no one showed any reluctance or saw any harm in jokingly touching the child's sexual parts." |

| | |
|---|---|
| 18th Century CE | Children were harshly punished for touching their own genitals. |
| | Cardinal Francois Joachim de Pierre de Bernis recalled being sexually molested by a nurse as a child. |
| | [Germany] One doctor reported that nursemaids and servants carried out "all sorts of sexual acts" on children "for fun." |
| 1896 | [Germany] Freud noticed "the connection between a history of childhood sexual trauma and psychological disturbance in adult life." |
| 1900 | According to psychoanalyst Robert Fleiss, "there were still people who believed venereal disease could be cured by means of sexual intercourse with children. |
| 1920 | [England] Author Virginia Woolf disclosed her incestuous relationship with her half-brother, George Duckworth, to the women of her Memoirs Club. |
| 1953 | [US] The Kinsey report on "Female Sexuality" was published. 25% of the women responding to Kinsey's questionnaire said "they had either had sex with adult men while they were children, or had been approached by men seeking sex." |
| 1970-1980 | [US] Women writers—Maya Angelou, Katherine Brady, and Charlotte Vale Allen—published their autobiographies and disclosed about the sexual abuse they experienced as children.[8] |
| Late 1970s | [Switzerland and US] Professionals in the behavioral and social science fields began to pay close attention to the sexual abuse of children. |
| 1983 | [US] The first Roman Catholic priest was prosecuted for the sexual abuse of over 70 boys. |

# APPENDIX 4

# *Denominational and Organizational Contacts*

## THE EPISCOPAL CHURCH

The Episcopal Church Center
815 Second Avenue
New York, NY 10017
(212) 867-8400

Department of Women in Mission and Ministry
(800) 334-7627 x5442

## EVANGELICAL LUTHERAN CHURCH IN AMERICA

Evangelical Lutheran Church in America
8765 West Higgins Road
Chicago, IL 60631-4187

Child and Family Ministries
(312) 380-2687

Commission for Church in Society
(312) 380-2705

Department of Christian Education
(312) 380-2557

# LUTHERAN CHURCH-MISSOURI SYNOD

LCMS
1333 S. Kirkwood Rd.
St. Louis, MO 63122-7295

Child Abuse Task Force Contact
(314) 965-9917 x 1244

# THE PRESBYTERIAN CHURCH USA

The Presbyterian Church, USA
100 Witherspoon Street
Louisville, KY 40202-1369
(502) 569-5000

Child Advocacy Office
(502) 569-5482

Child Advocacy Project
(502) 569-5792

Department of Social Justice and Peacemaking
(502) 569-5793

# THE ROMAN CATHOLIC CHURCH IN AMERICA

The National Conference of Catholic Bishops
Washington, DC
(202) 542-3000

Department of Religious Education
(202) 541-3185

Department of Domestic and Social Development
(202) 541-3185

The complete 90-page report of the Canadian Bishops, published in booklet form, can be ordered for $5.50 from: Publications Service, Canadian Conference of Catholic Bishops, 90 Parent Avenue, Ottawa, Ontario K1N 7B1, Canada.

# THE UNITED CHURCH OF CHRIST

United Church of Christ in America
700 Prospect Ave.
Cleveland, OH 44115-1100
(216) 736-3800

Department of Education and Publications
(216) 870-3454

Coordinating Center for Women
(216) 736-2150

Board of Homeland Ministries
(216) 870-2100

Office for Church and Society
(216) 736-2174

# THE UNITARIAN UNIVERSALIST ASSOCIATION

The Unitarian Universalist Association
25 Beacon Street Boston, MA 01208
(617) 742-2100

Department of Religious Education
(617) 742-2100 x 370

Department of Social Justice
(617) 742-2100

The Unitarian Universalist Service Committee
130 Prospect St.
Cambridge, MA 02139
(617) 868-6600

# THE UNITED METHODIST CHURCH

The United Methodist Church
General Board of Church and Society
100 Maryland Avenue, N.E.

Washington, DC 20002
(202) 488-5600

Department of Ministry and Human Community
(202) 488-5600

General Board of Global Ministries
Department of Ministries with Women and Families
(212) 870-3600

# THE NATIONAL COUNCIL OF THE CHURCHES OF CHRIST IN THE USA

475 Riverside Drive
New York, NY 10155

# NATIONAL AGENCIES

CHILDREN'S DEFENSE FUND
122 C. Street NW
Washington, DC 20001
(202) 628-8787

THE NATIONAL COMMITTEE FOR THE PREVENTION OF CHILD ABUSE
322 South Michigan Avenue, Suite 950
Chicago, IL 60604
(312) 663-3520

THE NATIONAL RESOURCE CENTER ON CHILD SEXUAL ABUSE
107 Lincoln Street
Huntsville, AL 35801
(205) 534-6868

NATIONAL VICTIM CENTER
2111 Wilson Boulevard, Suite 300
Arlington, VA 22201
(703) 276-2880

## PROFESSIONAL ORGANIZATION

APSAC
American Professional Society on the Abuse of Children
332 South Michigan, Suite 1600
Chicago, IL 60604
(312) 554-0166

# APPENDIX 5

# *Sample Sermons*

---

## "Not In My Family: Some Issues of Sexual Abuse"

*Reverend Libbie Deverich Stoddard*
*Unitarian Universalist Fellowship*
*Lafayette, Indiana*

What I want to do first is to set the stage a little bit: to "talk about" what I'm going to talk about. This topic, sexual abuse, will be, for some of you, hard to listen to, hard to believe, hard to understand. But the fact is that some subjects cannot be made "nice" or "easy," no matter what we do—that is, not if we really want to address them. Also, I am wearing my pulpit robe this morning. I am wearing it not to distance or separate myself from you, but as a visible reminder that I am speaking out of, and to, the religious institution.

I know that some of you in the congregation have been sexually abused, or that someone in your family has been. Maybe you don't even know about it yet. I know this not because you have told me, and not because it somehow shows on your faces. It does not show. My knowledge comes from statistics: one out of three or four women, one out of six or seven men, was sexually abused before the age of 18. In fact, the statistics changed even as I wrote them: a book on male victims says that there is increasing evidence that boys and girls are molested in about the same numbers. Sexual abuse happens to children in professors' families, doctors' families, and lawyers' families as well as in the families of sanitation workers and assembly-line workers. Sexual abuse happens to children in rich families as well as families on public assistance. It happens to children of all races, all religious traditions, and all countries in the world.

Sexual abuse does not include only victims or survivors. It also includes abusers. Most abusers are men, but not all: some women also abuse children—their own, someone else's. So there may well be some of you who have sexually abused a child—maybe once, maybe twice; maybe you continue to do it. If this is or has been your situation, I say clearly that those acts are wrongful acts, and that they must stop; I say also that I will do my best to direct you to the most competent help I know of.

Sexual abuse is a term with a variety of connotations. Generally, it is used to refer to any form of sexual activity involving two—or more—persons, where sexual gratification is desired only by the older, stronger, more powerful person; where there is a disparity in age or in the ability to control, or consent to the situation; where there is coercion, real or implied. Coercion has many faces: we are coercive when we bodily remove a child from an electric outlet, or when we take a bicycle away for a week from our child who has ridden carelessly in the street.

Children are accustomed to being protected by adults; their lives literally depend on the protection that surrounds them: protection from danger, and the positive protections of food, shelter, clothing, medical care. But there are the ugly coercions: those exclusively of power and role. Do this because I say so; do this because I am your parent, babysitter, doctor, lawyer, teacher, and yes, minister. Five years ago, three or four ministers from a variety of denominations were indicted on child-molesting charges in a nearby city. In the past few months, I have spoken with both men and women who were molested by members of the clergy—again, a variety of religious backgrounds and traditions.

About five years ago, I began to respond to those wrongful acts, first by reading widely and intentionally on the subject of sexual abuse. After some months of reading, I gave a sermon about what I had learned. Following the service, a woman in the congregation came up to ask if I knew of any local support groups for women who had been sexually abused. I told her that, to my knowledge, there were none. She said, "Let's start one"; and so we did. The courage of that woman, and of the 30, 40, maybe 60 women and a few men with whom I have spoken in these four years, never fails to amaze and encourage me. There is no question that what I say today is *their* sermon; it reflects their courage and their hard-won self-respect, which they have given me the privilege to speak aloud. There is no way that four years, many books, many personal stories can be compressed into one Sunday service. What I have chosen to do in the sermon is to focus on three questions that are often asked about sexual abuse: 1) Did it really happen? 2) Why don't—or didn't—they tell? and 3) Why don't—or can't—they forgive and forget?

Did it really happen? Four years ago, when I spoke here about a minister's conviction, that was one of the first questions asked, "Did he really do it . . . or was it maybe?" I like to think that this kind of doubting question arises out of horror rather than out of distrust. It is common, and normal, for us to respond to bad news with "No!" or "You're joking!" or "That can't be true!" These denial statements are acceptable between adults, but to respond to a child in that way is not helpful. The child must be presumed to be telling the truth about sexual abuse. It is not that children don't ever deny, mislead, imagine, and forget: "No, I didn't take the cookies . . . I didn't take the coins from your purse . . . No, the teacher didn't give me my report card today . . . Sure, I made my bed, did all my homework . . . His mother *said* I could stay for dinner and for overnight and all next week, too . . ."

But these statements are well within the range of a child's normal activities and bodily growth and development. Despite advertisements and the excesses of television movies, most children do not understand, for instance, why an adult would want to touch or kiss the child's genitals; or why an adult would want the child to fondle, kiss or take in his or her mouth the adult's genitals. Adults who are beginning to remember and to tell about their experiences of being abused often come up against the psychological concept that what you say you hate, you really like; if you say your father abused you, it's probably a fantasy left over from the Oedipal stage. I am perfectly willing to grant that we humans often distort our experiences and our memories, and that we often repress the desire for or knowledge of what we deeply or secretly want. But for the most part, I think fantasies are daydreams of *pleasure*: we'll win the lottery; win the most beautiful or the most handsome lover; have new furniture for every room in the house—and a swimming pool—write the best book, grow the best tomatoes. The women I have spoken with have not found abuse to be a happy part of the imaginings. Many women and men go to great lengths to forget that the abuse ever happened; many have full or partial amnesia about the abusive events for as long as 20, 30 or 50 years. As adults, celibate or not, we understand that we are sexual beings, intended to be that way, and that our sexuality is intended to be pleasurable.

Sexual abuse, on the other hand, includes a minimum of pleasure and a maximum of pain. If the abuser is a member of the family, or lives in the house, or has access to the house, the victim is never safe from being touched, grabbed, molested. In many hospitals, current practice is for children never to have treatments in their own rooms or in their own beds: even sick children are given safe places. One's own bed is dangerous. So are the bathroom, kitchen, workroom, barn. This is not the material of childlike fantasies. Abuse really happens.

The second question is, "Why don't—or didn't—they tell?" Even the way the question is phrased is revealing: "Why don't *they* tell?" No one ever says, "Why don't—or didn't—we ask?" Even now, even therapists are still apt to say things like, "Oh well, that happened a long time ago and you're over it now, aren't you." And the words are a statement, not a question. Parents and teachers say, "Mean what you say and say what you mean" (with a silent corollary appended) "unless it's something I don't want to hear." And children know very well what their parents are willing to hear. Currently there is much emphasis on the "yell and tell" approach, stressing that if a child runs away or tells an adult, the abuse will stop, or perhaps, never happen in the first place. Unfortunately, that is not always true. Certainly it is not true often enough. It is well to warn our children about men lurking behind billboards, and about kindly strangers in cars. But how do we warn our children about their fathers, stepfathers, grandfathers, brothers, uncles—or about their mothers and aunts—on whom they are dependent for food, clothes, shelter, and love? How do we warn them about their parents' close friends, about their babysitters? How do we *realistically* tell our children not to be afraid of someone who is twice their height or three or four times their weight?

Why don't they tell? Because they *are* afraid, afraid of being hurt, even of being killed. Many women have told me of beatings that they endured when they tried either to avoid or to comply with the abuser's demands. If begging "Please, no!" gets you thrown to the floor, injured enough to require medical atttention, what worse thing might happen to you if you tell the doctor or nurse—in front of your abuser—that you really didn't fall down the cellar stairs? And will you even attempt to refuse the next act of sexual abuse? How do you say to medical personnel, treating you for rectal tears, that you submitted to anal intercourse in the hopes that you wouldn't become pregnant by your abuser . . . still another time? And after the tissues have healed, what risk will you choose in the future: anal, vaginal, or oral intercourse? Why don't they tell? Because of the beatings, the injuries, the pain, the threats. "If you tell, I'll kill you." "If you tell, you'll be sent away." "If you tell, you'll break up the family."

Children don't know that sexual abuse has already broken up the family. Not legally broken up, perhaps, but the appropriate and nourishing ties of trust and protection are already ruptured. And too often—not always, but too often—it is the child who has to move out of the home when the abuser is part of the family system. The books I've read say that it is the abuser who has to leave, but it does not always happen that way. It is far easier to remove the child. So the child goes into protective care—away from the abuser, true—but away from the supportive family members, away from what is familiar and known. Away, perhaps to a different school district. And if transportation to the original school is arranged, how does a child (even an older child) explain this to classmates? Some women, looking back, say that school was, for them, a safe place. Even though they couldn't talk about their experiences, the abuser couldn't get at them for a certain number of hours each day. Yet school, at the upper grade levels at any rate, has one particular trap for girls, maybe not for boys. Gym classes: getting undressed, taking showers. A number of women have spoken of their fears: "Classmates will be able to tell, just by looking at me, that I've been abused." "My body must show the effects of those acts of anal, oral, vaginal intercourse." My abuser got me pregnant; stretch marks will show." Or, "My abuser got me pregnant; everyone will know I've had an abortion!"

Maybe the most difficult, most painful answer to "But why don't they tell?" is part threat and part fact: "No one will believe you." The threat, even from someone outside the family, is enough to keep a child silenced for years, regardless of whether or not the parent or parents would have been supportive and protective. But too often, still too often, responses from family members, including siblings, are angry or actively unhelpful: "Submit now and leave later." "Don't be so prudish!" "You're only making this up because we didn't let you go to the movies with your friends last weekend." "You must have led him on." "He/she is a respected person in the community and wouldn't have done that!" "He only *touched* you." "Why can't you think of anything else . . . Why are you continually fussing about it?" I know of women, in and out of this community, who tried to talk about the abuse to parents, teachers, guidance counselors, religious leaders and even protective services, and were not believed. After a while, they stopped talking.

And there are inner reasons for expecting disbelief. Women and men both often report that they feared they would not be believed because some part of the abuse was pleasurable to them: usually gentle fondling or tickling games; perhaps, despite their fear of the abuser, they reached orgasm; or in some situations, the abuser gave them extra attention or special gifts. But no matter how gentle the touch, how respected or generous the abuser, sexual contact between adult and child is a wrongful act. It distorts the child's sense of trust, it violates personal boundaries, and it seriously damages the child's development, whether physical, emotional, or psychological.

But why don't they forget? Why don't they forgive the abuser? Part of the answer lies in what I have just said: Sexual abuse distorts childhood's growth and trust. Increasingly, women and men discover that the abuse has affected nearly all aspects of their lives. They suffer from distrust of close relationships and confusion about boundaries and personal rights; they fear raising children, especially children of the same sex as the abuser. They experience an inability to study and concentrate, or perfectionism and a sense of overreaching personal responsibility; they suffer from self-destructive acts and practices, including alcoholism, drug use, eating disorders, promiscuity, prostitution, attempts at suicide, and suicide completed.

Psychotic episodes and, some practitioners believe, multiple personality disorders often result from the attempts to wall off or guard against the abusive acts. And there are the flashbacks: certain music, odors, food; certain ways of being touched, approached—all innocent or neutral in themselves—that may be a sudden reminder of an earlier, painful experience. If any of you saw the movie "Nuts" with Barbara Streisand, you saw flashbacks. How can they forget? The experiences have tentacles in one's entire life. The life process, for those who have been abused, is ideally a matter of reassessing the experiences, putting them into perspective, not denying them, but also not giving them more than their share of psychic space.

Allied to forgetting is forgiving. To forgive is a demand that comes from both the religious and psychological communities. I won't attempt to speak for the psychological communities, but I will venture into speaking for—at least some of—the religious community. Only a few of the women I've spoken with or read about over the past four years have had any help from their congregations, their clergy, or their sacred scriptures. I think that some of these difficulties stem from the way Scripture is often taught. For instance, this beautiful passage from Deuteronomy: "The Lord will love you and bless you and multiply you. He will bless the issue of your wombs and the produce of your soil . . . There shall be no sterile male or female among you, or among your livestock . . . The Lord will ward off from you all sickness." At one level, the words are clear enough: if you are good enough, obedient enough, you will be protected. You will not be sterile from gonorrhea contracted from your abuser when you were five years old; you will not get AIDS from forced anal intercourse; you will not have to fight against daily, hourly, suicidal impulses and desires.

I think it is the responsibility of the religious community to be clear that words such as those I just read are to be understood not solely as words of immediate and personal experience, but also as words of group hope and group faith and group belonging. They are words of religious community, not of religious isolation or individualism. "Religion" means "that which binds together," but narrow and individualized Scriptural translations do not bind together; they tear apart. Sexually-abused women raised in Catholic families struggle all their lives to make sense of the fact that their parents, vigorously disapproving of abortion, yet took them to have abortions at the age of 12, 13, 14. Protestant women and men struggle to make sense of the fact that their often very strict religious families appeared so warm and loving in public—some even wearing special clothing that marked them as members of a particular religious sect—but at home the children were sexually abused and beaten by one or both parents, perhaps grandparents as well. Jewish women and men suffer from the traditional understanding that Jewish men are gentler and kinder than non-Jewish men, and post-Holocaust, repeatedly ask the question, "After such horror, does my suffering even matter?"

Forgiveness, then, within the religious community often comes to mean to the survivors of sexual abuse another way that society says to them, "Do this, feel this, on *my* schedule, not yours." "Do this [forgive the abuser] because it is the right thing to do." "Do this [forgive the abuser] so that *I* don't need to listen to your pain." Marie Fortune is an ordained Protestant minister whose work is in the field of domestic violence. I attended a workshop she gave in May 1988. To victims of abuse, and to those who work with the abused, Marie was clear, outspoken, and scriptural: "Don't forgive until or unless you are ready to and want to. And if you are never ready, that's OK, too." Then she added, very slowly, very religiously, "Forgiveness is God's gift to the victim, not to the abuser."

What Marie meant, in part, was that the victim's first and deepest need is to learn—to *begin* to learn—to forgive herself or himself. To forgive oneself for running away, or for staying; for telling about the abuse—or for not telling; for years, decades, of promiscuity or prostitution; for losing control and vomiting at moments of terror and disgust; for crying—and for learning not to cry; for abortions, chosen or forced; for experiencing, even seeking, the body's pleasurable sensations; for surviving, above all—and by any and all means necessary. Until we as clergy and congregations understand forgiveness in that way, we do well to keep our mouths shut on the subject.

Where to go from here? What more to learn, what more to do? I can't answer that question for you as individuals— even as this religious community—or as members of other religious communities. I do ask a few things, though—that you keep in mind the statistics: 1 out of every 3 or 4 women you meet *anywhere* and one out of 6 or 7—or perhaps even 3 or 4 men you meet *anywhere* were sexually abused before the age of 18. Remember, too, that sexual abuse of children is not about love; it is about power and control and secrecy. And be kind to people: you cannot know their pain by how they dress or how they look or how they speak or how—and if—they pray.

## "As I Have Loved You "
### John 15:9-17

*Reverend Dudley C. Rose*
*North-Prospect United Church of Christ*
*Cambridge, Massachusetts*

As the Father has loved me, so I have loved you; abide in my love. If you keep my commandments, you will abide in my love, just as I have kept my Father's commandments and abide in his love. I have said these things to you so that my joy may be in you, and that your joy may be complete. This is my commandment, that you love one another as I have loved you. No one has greater love than this, to lay down one's life for one's friends. You are my friends if you do what I command you. I do not call you servants any longer, because the servant does not know what the master is doing; but I have called you friends, because I have made known to you everything that I have heard from my Father. You did not choose me but I chose you, and I appointed you to go and bear fruit, fruit that will last, so that the Father will give you whatever you ask him in my name. I am giving you these commands so that you may love one another. (NRSV)

There are subjects that are difficult to talk about, and this morning I want to start off by talking about one of them. In 1986 the American Humane Association reported that 140,000 cases of child sexual abuse were reported to professionals in the United States in that year. (Angelica 1991) It is a generally accepted fact that the number of cases reported is a small fraction of the actual incidents. 140,000 cases of child sexual abuse in one year in this country, and that number is likely to be a small percentage. To put that number in perspective, 60,000 Americans lost their lives in all the Vietnam War.

This comparison is interesting on a number of counts. First, many of us remember how the loss of life in the Vietnam War tore the country in two. For years, it seemed, the War began every newscast. Battle reports, strategies, political posturing were prevalent. But the thing that finally turned it all upside down was the count of the dead and the seemingly endless images of body bags being loaded and unloaded from airplanes. It became too much for the nation to bear. And finally we left Vietnam, not because of victory or defeat, but because there was no longer the will to pay the price.

The price was high. 60,000 lives lost and many more wounded. But isn't it incredible that almost two-and-a-half times that many children that we know about, 140,000, are sexually abused in this country every year, and there is hardly a murmur of indignation?

There are many reasons, no doubt. Perhaps the largest is the one that makes me uncomfortable preaching about this, and maybe makes you uncomfortable listening: It is just too offensive for the mind. And since it happens most often in homes and families, where the cries don't penetrate the walls, where often the cries do not even escape from the mouths of the children, too confused and scared to death and horrified to know what to do, because the injury often isn't readily visible, it is easier to ignore than other forms of violence. Because it is so distasteful a topic and because we don't have to see the 140,000 victims bleeding before us, we can more easily believe it is not true. But it is true.

And the injury runs deep. It lasts a long time, often a lifetime. Again, since the wounds may be internal, it may be tempting to think the victims are OK, that they get over it; as some say, "They're only kids; they'll grow up and be fine."

All the evidence suggests something else.

For some children, it is like dying. And some do die, often at their own hands, perhaps many years later. And possibly the most disturbing thing is that those who perpetrate child sexual abuse almost always were themselves abused as children. What emerges, then, is a dramatic picture of cause and effect in which, from generation to generation, abused children become abusers. And on and on it goes, an endless chain.

The succession of abuse from one generation to the next is the shadow side of the message in this morning's scripture: "As the Father has loved me, so I have loved you."

It goes on to say: "This is my commandment, that you love one another as I have loved you." And what we see is that this commandment may act as a description of the way things are as much as it does an admonition. It suggests that the way we have been treated can have enormous influence on how we will treat others. It says: "Love one another as I have loved you." It means: From the love you have experienced from me, from the way I have treated you, you have learned how to treat one another with love.

For those who have experienced something else, who have experienced abuse, for example, instead of love, the process, unfortunately, works just as well.

So what are the roles for the church to play? Or another way of asking the question, why bring up this unseemly topic in church?

First of all, because the facts and the prevalence are shocking. In 1953, Alfred Kinsey in his famous research found that one in four women had experienced sexual contact with an adult male or had been approached by men for sexual contact while they were children. In a more random sample in 1983, Diana Russell found the number to be 38%. Almost always the perpetrator was known to the child, most often a close family member. (Angelica 1991)

So, one reason to bring it up is that it is a significant issue in the lives of so many people that it would be a putting of our collective heads in the sand to assume that our church community could be unaffected. Thus, it is a pastoral issue. There are likely some of us who have been directly affected. It would be unfair to pretend it is not so.

Related to that reason is another: Where better than a church to speak of such things? If the church becomes too delicate, too concerned with propriety to speak such things, it sends a clear message. It says don't bring your real problems, your real pain, your real life here. It says what many survivors of abuse have heard all too often and all too loudly: Cover it up; Don't talk about it; Pretend it never happened.

What I am speaking about here goes far beyond talking of issues of sexual abuse of children. It is a broader question of what is acceptable to bring to church. Is church a place for your Sunday-best appearance, not only as far as your clothes are concerned, but in every way? Is church about wearing masks of propriety? Is it about pretending? Or is it a place where all that we are, our deepest wounds and our profoundest hopes, is given room? Often enough the church has become irrelevant when it has told people that their greatest reason for coming is unwelcome.

So, what am I proposing? Am I suggesting that the church should be a place full of groans and mourning, a place where you can come on Sunday morning and get really depressed? Well, that would be pretty awful, wouldn't it?

But perhaps the greatest wisdom of the Christian faith is that it sets the cross and resurrection side by side. It links them directly together. And in doing that, in placing Good Friday and Easter Sunday at the center of its theology, it says that even the darkest of moments contains the promise of rebirth. And another point that is often missed, I think, is that it says we can be joyful even when some things are still painful. It gives us the freedom to quit pretending that everything has to be okay to be able to enjoy the wonder and the beauty of life, or the sunshine of a day like this one. The juxtaposition of the cross and the resurrection tells us of the bittersweet mixture that life is, and gives us permission to accept the ambiguity without opting for either "everything is awful" or "everything is wonderful."

That's part of what I'm proposing by suggesting we not be too dainty about what we talk about in church. But there is something that goes even farther.

"As the Father has loved me, so I have loved you: Abide in my love . . . This is my commandment, that you love one another as I have loved you."

One of the daunting things about child sexual abuse is the way it perpetuates itself. The victim is wounded enough that in adulthood he or she often becomes the perpetrator. But this is not an isolated theme. All across the spectrum of human experience we pass behavior from generation to generation, and much of it is hurtful and keeps us from being whole. And this is not simply modern theory. Thousands of years ago the Bible expressed it as the sins of the father being passed through the generations. It has long been recognized that much gets transmitted from lifetime to lifetime, depending on how people are treated, and all too often they experience painful, even abusive lessons.

All of this points to what may be the most important role of all for the church. It can be disheartening to recognize the pain with which people have been caused to live and to recognize the ways it continues to be transmitted. How can the cycle be broken?

The church at its best has a way, I think. The theories at which we have looked and this morning's scripture seem to suggest that we will learn to love one another to the extent that we have experienced love ourselves. The church is one place, perhaps one of the very few, where that can be worked out. To the degree that we are all human, it will never happen perfectly. But if we see ourselves located in the middle of Jesus' commandment—That you love one another as I have loved you—some wonderful things can begin to happen.

We can welcome everyone, including each of us. We can allow the truth to be spoken in church, so that those who come hear that they can be loved today, rather than hear what they have heard already too often, that their real selves are not acceptable. It can happen in sermons. It can happen at groups. It can happen in the right hand of fellowship. It can happen at coffee hour. It doesn't even have to be a direct conversation, for it is an attitude more than anything else. It is an attitude that will show itself by whether the smile is genuine, and the handshake sincere.

And as we do these things with one another, a miracle begins to shape itself. For new lessons are learned. Old wounds begin to heal. And old cycles begin to crumble. For just as we have passed on the hurt we have experienced, we now have the opportunity to pass on to one another the care and the healing we have experienced. This is the mandate of the church community. And no other place can do it as well.

"Abide in my love . . . This is my commandment, that you love one another as I have loved you." So said Jesus. So may we do.

Thanks be to God. Amen.

## "Shattering the Silence: Incest"

### Reverend Jayne Rose Brewer

(Rev. Brewer is affiliated with the American Baptist Church in the Boston Area. This sermon was specifically written for inclusion in *Sermons Seldom Heard: Women Proclaim Their Lives*, edited by Annie Lally Milhaven.)[9]

There is an epidemic in our country that is devastating millions of lives. It affects every family. It is prevalent in every culture and socio-economic group. It is present in the church. It is incest.

The statistics tell us that one in three women have been sexually abused during their childhood by fathers, brothers, sometimes mothers, or other trusted family members or friends. Children are being terrorized by their families. The people they should be able to trust the most are proving to be the most untrustworthy. These are children we are talking about. Defenseless children, at the mercy of the adults around them. The little girl in your Sunday School class. The child who played the angel in the church play. They seem normal enough. You would never suspect they were being subjected to any kind of harm, let alone the brutal violence of sexual abuse. They would probably not tell you anything was going on if you were to ask them. They have been taught well to keep the family's horrible secret. To protect those who are harming them. To deny that they are being harmed in any way. They learned to stop asking questions. They were told it was their fault, that they were bad; they were bribed to keep the secret. The "special treatment" from their abuser is sometimes the only affection given by any family member. Perhaps they were threatened with more physical harm to themselves or to someone else in the family. A father will threaten to kill the mother if the child tells. All too often there is no one these defenseless children can turn to for help. And when they do, they are not believed. No one wants to hear that incest, violence against children, is so rampant in our society.

Including the church. The church where all can come for refuge. The church where love is proclaimed as available to all who seek God. The church where the subject of incest is even more taboo than in the rest of society.

We, in the church, have created numerous myths about the "happy Christian family." We developed an atmosphere where raising questions about the family's behavior is impossible. The father's position in the family is practically sacred. No one wants to hear that the deacon, the Sunday school teacher, the preacher, sexually abuses his daughter or son. And perhaps neighbor's children as well. Should a child have the courage to tell that she is being sexually abused by her father, she is usually greeted with shocked looks of disbelief. And more often than not, the church's protection surrounds the abusive parent, pointing the finger of accusation at the child for making up such lies about her father. No, the church does not have a very good record of listening to the pain of its daughters—a situation in direct contrast to the Scripture in Matthew 7:7-8.

The Scripture says, "Ask, and it shall be given you; seek, and ye shall find; knock, and it shall be opened unto you; For every one that asketh receiveth; and s/he that seeketh findeth; and to them that knocketh it shall be opened." However, the message coming from incestuous families, and supported by the church, is that children being sexually abused, are not to question their fathers' behavior. They are not to seek help outside the family structure, or in it. They are not to knock on the closed family door, let alone expect it to be opened to let them out. They are expected to live in silence. Keeping the family secret. Forever.

As adults, women are discovering that telling the family secret is still not safe. The family doesn't want to hear the pain any more now than it ever did. The church asks women to be quiet about their pain, not to speak out for fear of embarrassing themselves, their families, or the church. And God forbid that the millions of women who were subjected to terror and abuse as children should knock on the door of the church seeking solace. No, the church is not equipped to handle the pain of its daughters for it is structured in such a way as to hear no evil, speak no evil, and see no evil within the "happy Christian family."

We in the church have developed the ability not to hear what we do not want to hear; to filter out that which does not fit into the way we would like life to be. If we don't want to hear it, we don't hear it. If we don't want to see it, we don't see it. If we don't want to think about it, we don't think about it. We, in effect, have closed our minds to the pain women throughout the country are voicing. To understand how we in the church have been able to shut out the anguish of the women in the church isn't so difficult. To deny reality is something with which incest survivors are all too familiar.

Incest victims are programmed not to feel pain, not to see the destructive behavior around them, not to hear the cries of anguish from their own lips, not to think about what is happening to them. To "see no evil, hear no evil, speak no evil" was added "feel no pain" and "do not think about the evil around you." The programming was intense. The victims' parents had a lot at stake. It was vital to their need not to see, hear, speak, think, or feel, that their victims accept the programming. And the victims did accept it. They did it to survive.

As we think about what parents have done to the minds and bodies of their children, our minds can't seem to expand enough to grasp the horror and terror to which these children were subjected. No wonder their minds rejected reality, denied their feelings, and learned to pretend to live in a world that didn't exist. They learned not to question. They learned it was better not to think. Their minds couldn't even begin to grapple with the discrepancies between how they were experiencing life and what they were told life was all about, both in the family and in the church. Day by day, moment by moment they were programmed to ignore their reality. Instead, they were to see something that was not there, namely, a "happy Christian family." It is a long, slow process for women to break down so many years of firm, sometimes blatant, many times insidious teaching, intent on making them blind and ignorant of the reality around them.

No wonder that when a woman is finally able to break the silence, she seems to direct an uncontrolled explosion of anger and hatred toward her abusers. Quickly the church steps in to smother the feelings, for the church has as much trouble handling true feelings as the family does. The church calls on women to love their enemies, to forgive their abusers. It is time the church realizes that love and forgiveness are inappropriate responses, especially when the behavior has never been confessed or repented of. It is time for the church to stop contributing to the silencing of women in pain. It is time that we realize the sexual abuse of our children will not stop until we call the abusers to account for their actions.

How many times does a child have to be molested or raped before she is allowed to be angry? When do those who are abused get to call their abusers to account for the violence against them? Why do the abusers get to be angry, venting their anger in innumerable ways, but those who are being hurt are expected to stifle their anger and hope the abusers will stop hurting them of their own accord? When do the victims get to ask why the abusers behaved as they did? When do they get to seek help, comfort, and protection? When do they get to knock on the doors that have been slammed in their faces with some hope they might be opened?

There is an epidemic in our country that claims thousands of victims each year, while infecting still millions more. The time has come to break the code of silence surrounding the presence of incest in our society. The church must take a stand against this reign of terror that destroys so many lives. It is time for the church to listen, to no longer deny the existence of incest in our midst and its devastating effect on millions of lives—including the lives of those in the church.

The victims of incest are asked to live in a damning silence. There is never an appropriate time to tell of the pain, the hurt, the fear, the humiliation they have lived with all their lives. Few people have any problem with being horrified when a child is touched in inappropriate ways or raped by a stranger. Yet, children are subjected to all manner of sexual violence in their homes, and no one wants to hear about it. Victims and survivors need to be free from the damning silence. It is the responsibility of the church, which claims to be a refuge for all who are weary, to take the victims and survivors of incest, who are weary to the point of exhaustion, into their midst.

It is time for the church to allow the Scriptures to live in the lives of incest victims and survivors. Out of the silence voices are beginning to be heard. The church must begin to hear these voices, not silence them. As women tentatively begin to ask why they were subjected to totally unacceptable sexual abuse from their family, we in the church must support them. We must hear their questions and insist they be answered. As women seek to rebuild their lives, to escape the terror of the past, the church must support them in their endeavor. As women knock on the door of the church, asking to be heard, the door must be opened. It is time the church stopped contributing to the silence.

Victims of incest had a right to be loved as children, not neglected and sexually abused. They had a right to have their needs met, to feel safe and nurtured, not always living in fear and giving their hearts' blood to the adult who demanded that they supply their needs. It is time for the church to stand with the victims and call a halt to incestuous behavior. It will not be easy as no one wants to hear the daughters' pain. They want to go on pretending that life is fine, to blame the victims for the abuse. If the church cannot open its doors to these daughters, the daughters will be forced to seek solace elsewhere. Most do not want to leave the church. Most want the words of Jesus to live for them as well as for others. The church must let these words bring the healing that Jesus intended.

It will take time for victims and survivors of incest to trust the church. The church, in the past, has kept women silent. The daughters are now beginning to call the church to account for its behavior, just as they are challenging their abusers. All too often the church is failing the test, continuing to show itself to be untrustworthy. If the daughters are to be reconciled to the church, they must be able to tell their stories and be heard, not condemned. The words of Jesus, "ask, seek, knock," must free women to break through the silence that surrounded them in the past and still threatens to smother them in the present. The church must learn to hear the voices of its daughters in new ways, to see the terror in which they live, to speak out against the fathers and brothers, to acknowledge the feelings of fear and bewilderment with which the daughters live, to think about ways to change family systems that are taking a devastating toll on the lives of those who are being sexually abused. It is time the church became an advocate for the abused, not the abuser.

The church is faced with an important decision. It has to decide whether to start believing the daughters when they voice their pain and despair. What the church decides will have an impact on millions of lives. The church can stem the epidemic of incest in our country. Everything it teaches about the love and goodness of God demands that it do so.

---

*Jayne Rose Brewer was sexually abused in childhood by her father and two older brothers.*

# Notes

**Preface**
1. Prescott Browning Wintersteen, *Christology in American Unitarianism: 19th and 20th Century Unitarian Theologians.* (Boston: Unitarian Universalist Christian Fellowship, 1977), 93.
2. *Ibid.*

**Chapter One**
1. Steve, a victim of sexual abuse during childhood. He doesn't like the word "survivor." Page One Productions, *Massachusetts Law in Plain Talk* (Lowell, MA 1989), videocassette.
2. Catherine, survivor. Written account shared with the author.
3. Jane Walsh, Assistant District Attorney, interview by author, 8 November 1989, tape recording. Middlesex County District Attorney's Office, Child Abuse Prosecution Unit, Somerville, MA. 1990 statistics were added to the data provided by Assistant District Attorney Walsh.
4. The prosecutor and the ethicist were interviewed by the author on 17 December 1990 in Cambridge, Massachusetts.

**Chapter Two**
1. Susan, survivor. Written account shared with the author.
2. Annamarie, survivor. Written account shared with the author.
3. Senator John Kerry, "Instead We Are Talking About War," *Congressional Record,* Vol. 137, No. 7, (January 11, 1991).
4. City room reporter, telephone interview by author, 7 February 1991, Boston, *The Boston Globe,* Boston.
5. Alexander Reid, "Scholars urge quest for cure to violence," *The Boston Sunday Globe,* 21 October, 1990.
6. David Finkelhor, telephone interview by author, 7 February 1991, Scarborough, ME.
7. Linda Meyer Williams, "Adult Memories of Childhood Abuse: Preliminary Findings from a Longitudinal Study," *The Advisor* Vol. 5, No. 3, (Summer 1992).
8. Mary Brown of the Washington State Coalition on Sexual Assault, telephone interview by author, 19 October 1992.
9. Rick Winters, Washington State Child Protective Services Research Department, telephone interview by author, 21 October, 1992.

10. California Consortium for the Prevention of Child Abuse, Sacramento, CA.
11. Massachusetts Children's Trust Fund.
12. Kellie Pini, *Case Analysis* (Somerville, MA: Middlesex County District Attorney's Office, Child Abuse Prosecution Unit, 5 January 1991).
13. Joan Grayson, editor, "Sexually Victimized Boys," *Virginia Child Protection Newsletter* Vol. 29 (Fall, 1989), 1- 2. VCPN cites Finkelhor's work, *Child Sexual Abuse: New Theory & Research.*
14. Gloria Steinem, dustcover review of *Secret Survivors*, by E. Sue Blume. Originally published by John Wiley & Sons, Inc., 1990.
15. Judith Herman, "Colloquium: Sexual Violence," Work in Progress, Wellesley College Stone Center, No. 83-5, 1984, 2.
16. *Ibid.*, 1.
17. David Finkelhor, telephone interview by author, 7 February 1991, Scarborough, ME. In his book, *A Sourcebook on Child Sexual Abuse*, David Finkelhor outlines selected studies. In Chapter 6 he points out some difficulties with previous research, and in Chapter 7 he makes suggestions for future study designs.
    With the exception of Kinsey's 1953 study, which documented child sexual abuse as a byproduct to the main focus of female sexuality, most of the research on child sexual abuse is relatively recent. According to the *Virginia Child Protection Newsletter*, the most common method of gathering random sample data seems to be questioning college students and adults about childhood sexual experiences. In *A Sourcebook on Child Sexual Abuse*, David Finkelhor indicated that some research has been conducted by use of standard psychological inventories, such as the MMPI and the California Psychological Inventory (p. 197). Some studies, according to Finkelhor, gathered their data via random-dialing telephone surveys (p. 33).
18. Edward Ross Maguire, *Profile of the Pedophile: A Critical Research Review* (Salisbury, MA: Independent research study) Section titled "Nature of Pedophilic Offenses."
19. David Finkelhor, telephone interview by author, 7 February 1991, Scarborough, ME.
20. Jane Walsh, Assistant District Attorney, interview by author, 22 November 1989, tape recording. Middlesex County District Attorney's Office, Child Abuse Prosecution Unit, Somerville, MA.
21. Thomas F. Reilly, Middlesex County District Attorney-elect, interview by author, 17 December 1990, Cambridge, MA, tape recording.
22. Hammalawa Saddhatissa, *Buddhist Ethics* (London: Wisdom Publications, 1987), 135.

23. Roland C. Summit, "The Child Abuse Accommodation Syndrome," *Child Abuse and Neglect,* Vol. 7 (1980), 189.
24. Alice Miller, *For Your Own Good* (New York: Farrar, Straus & Giroux Inc., 1983), 249.
25. Thomas F. Reilly, Middlesex County District Attorney-elect, interview by author, 17 December 1990, Cambridge, MA, tape recording.
26. Gail Elizabeth Wyatt and Gloria Johnson Powell, editors, *Lasting Effects of Child Sexual Abuse* (Newbury Park, 1988), "Hidden Victims, Hidden Pain," by Roland C. Summit, 57.
27. Professor Arthur J. Dyck, interview by author, 17 December 1990, Harvard Divinity School, Cambridge, MA, tape recording.
28. Gail Elizabeth Wyatt and Gloria Johnson Powell, editors, *Lasting Effects of Child Sexual Abuse* (Newbury Park, 1988), "Hidden Victims, Hidden Pain," by Roland C. Summit, 57.
29. Rachel Adelson, "Deadly Silence," *Voice,* 22 December 1989, 35.
30. Correspondence: Elizabeth Moore, LICSW to Jade C. Angelica, 14 March 1990.
31. Senator John Kerry, "Instead We Are Talking About War," *Congressional Record,* Vol. 137, No. 7 (January 11, 1991).
32. *Ibid.*

**Chapter Three**
1. Florence Rush, *The Best Kept Secret* (New York: McGraw-Hill, 1980) xii.
2. Kellie Pini, *Case Analysis* (Somerville, MA: Middlesex County District Attorney's Office, Child Abuse Prosecution Unit, 9 January 1992).
3. Elizabeth, survivor. Account shared with author by personal interview.
4. Jade C. Angelica, *We Are Not Alone . . . A Teenage Boy's Personal Account of Child Sexual Abuse from Disclosure through Prosecution and Treatment.* Excerpts from pre-publication manuscript, 1-3. "Joe" is a fictional character based on interviews with and observations of teenage victims of child sexual abuse within the Massachusetts Justice system.
5. Sally Jacobs, "Kingston confused, outraged in grief," *The Boston Sunday Globe,* 30 September 1990, 43.
6. Middlesex County Child Abuse Project, *The Child Abuse Reporting Law,* Theoharis K. Seghorn, "Myths & Facts About the Sexual Abuse Offender," (Cambridge: Middlesex County District Attorney's Office), 38.
7. Middlesex County Child Abuse Project, *The Child Abuse Reporting Law,* David Doolittle, "Is there an Offender Profile?" (Cambridge: Middlesex County District Attorney's Office), 39.

Roland Summit also comments on male child molesters in his article "The Child Abuse Accommodation Syndrome," p. 182. "The men implicated in most on-going sexual molestations are not [outwardly] perverted. They tend to be hard-working, devoted family men. They may be better educated, more law-abiding, and more religious than average."

8. Judith Herman, "Colloquium: Sexual Violence" Work in Progress, Wellesley College Stone Center, No. 83-05, 1984, 2.

9. Middlesex County Child Abuse Project, *The Child Abuse Reporting Law*, Theoharis K. Seghorn, "Myths and Facts about the Sexual Abuse Offender," (Cambridge: Middlesex County District Attorney's Office), 38.

10. Judith Herman, *Father-Daughter Incest* (Cambridge: Harvard University Press, 1981), 22.

11. Thomas F. Reilly, Middlesex County District Attorney-elect, interview by author, 17 December, 1990, Cambridge, MA, tape recording.

12. Linda T. Sanford, interview by author, 29 December 1989, Somerville, MA.

13. Lloyd de Mause, editor, *The History of Childhood: The Untold Story of Child Abuse* (New York: Peter Bedrick Books, 1988), 45.

14. Marie M. Fortune, *Sexual Violence: The Unmentionable Sin* (New York: The Pilgrim Press, 1983), 215.

15. Herman, *Father-Daughter Incest*, 129. In this quotation, the gender of the abuser was changed by the author from "father" to "parent;" the pronoun "he" was changed to "he/she." Dr. Herman's work was specific to fathers and daughters, however it should not be assumed that perpetrators are always male and victims always female. Much early research on child sexual abuse indicated that adult males were the perpetrators and girls were the victims. We now know that this is not always the case.

16. James M. Gustafson, *Ethics from a Theocentric Perspective* (Chicago: The University of Chicago Press, 1981), Premise of Chapter 5, "Marriage and Family."

17. Herman, *Father-Daughter Incest*, 202.

18. Thomas F. Reilly, Middlesex County District Attorney-elect, interview by author, 17 December 1990, Cambridge, MA, tape recording.

19. Gail Elizabeth Wyatt and Gloria Johnson Powell, editors, *Lasting Effects of Child Sexual Abuse* (Newbury Park, 1988), "Hidden Victims, Hidden Pain," by Roland C. Summit, 40.

20. *Ibid.*, 41.

21. Herman, *Father-Daughter Incest*, 202.

22. Hannah, survivor. Written account shared with author.

23. Herman, *Father-Daughter Incest,* 203.
24. Louise Armstrong, *Kiss Daddy Goodnight* (New York: Pocket Books, 1979), 275. Much of the early research in the area of child sexual abuse focused on girls; therefore, a number of quotations cited refer specifically to female victims through usage of the feminine pronouns "her" and "she." In some instances, the pronouns have been changed to reflect the inclusion of victimized boys. This quote was not changed because Louise Armstrong's book is the culmination of her interviews with 183 women. It is clearly a book written about and for women.
25. Sandra Butler, *Conspiracy of Silence: The Trauma of Incest* (San Francisco: New Glide Publications, 1978), 89.
26. Herman, *Father-Daughter Incest,* 27.
27. Roland C. Summit, "The Child Abuse Accommodation Syndrome," *Child Abuse and Neglect* Vol. 7 (1980) 183.
28. *Ibid.,* 182.
29. Film Distribution Center. *Breaking Silence.* (Seattle: Washington) videotape.
30. N. Dickon Reppucci, review of *With the Best of Intentions* (New York: The Guilford Press, 1991).
31. Jill Duerr Berrick and Neil Gilbert, *With the Best of Intentions* (New York: The Guilford Press, 1991).
32. Herman, *Father-Daughter Incest,* 27.
33. Linda T. Sanford, *But You Hide It So Well: Adult Survivors of Physical and Sexual Abuse* (Tape recording of lecture: June, 1988).
34. Linda T. Sanford, Page One Productions, *Massachusetts Law in Plain Talk,* Lowell, MA, 30 minutes, 1989, videocassette.
35. Jane Walsh Assistant District Attorney, interview by author, 22 November, 1989, tape recording. Middlesex County District Attorney's Office, Child Unit, Somerville, MA.
    Also, Linda T. Sanford, interview by author, 29 December 1989, Somerville, MA.
36. Bella English, "A Story of Betrayal," *The Boston Globe,* 13 June 1990. Ms. English wrote a column about a mother and her boyfriend who were being tried for the rape of the woman's five-year-old daughter. "The attorney representing the boyfriend kept the girl on the stand for about 40 minutes, with tedious questions that failed to shake her story. Much to [the attorney's] chagrin, undoubtedly, the girl revealed that she didn't like seeing her mother on visits, [the child was in foster care] that she was abused 'a lot of times' and that she told the mother and boyfriend to 'stop.'"
    Also, Linda T. Sanford, interview by author, 29 December 1989, Somerville, MA.
    In *The Best Kept Secret,* Florence Rush cites a cuneiform refer-

ence from a Sumerian clay tablet. "One tablet related the story of the god Enlil, who, when he encountered the goddess Ninlil bathing in a pure stream, desired her. The goddess, however, was unwilling:
"The lord speaks to her of intercourse. She is unwilling. Enlil speaks to her of intercourse. She is unwilling."
Ninlil politely explained her refusal.
"My vagina is too little. It knows not how to copulate. My lips are too small. They know not how to kiss." (Rush cites the work of Noah Kramer, *History Begins at Sumer* (New York: Doubleday Anchor, 1959), 85 - 86.

37. Herman, *Father-Daughter Incest*, 27.
38. Chloe, survivor. Tape recording and interview shared with author.
39. Summit, "The Child Abuse Accommodation Syndrome," 177.
40. Ellen Bass and Louise Thornton, editors, *I Never Told Anyone* (New York: Harper & Row, 1983), 158.
41. David B. Peters, *A Betrayal of Innocence* (Waco, Texas: Word Books, 1986), 47.
42. Rush, *The Best Kept Secret*. The entire premise of Ms. Rush's book, as clearly depicted by the title, is about the historical and current silence of both victims and non-victims in regard to child sexual abuse.
43. Bass and Thornton, *I Never Told Anyone*, 50.
44. Jon R. Conte, *A Look at Child Sexual Abuse* (Chicago: National Committee for the Prevention of Child Abuse, 1986), 24.
45. Bass and Thornton, *I Never Told Anyone*, 158.
46. Jane Walsh, Assistant District Attorney, interview by author, 22 November 1989, tape recording. Middlesex County District Attorney's Office, Child Unit, Somerville, MA.
    Also, Kellie Pini, *Case Analysis* (Somerville, MA: Middlesex County District Attorney's Office, Child Unit, 5 January 1991).
47. Thomas Reilly, Middlesex County District Attorney-elect, interview by author, 17 December 1991, Cambridge, MA, tape recording.
48. *Ibid.*
49. Kellie Pini, Middlesex County District Attorney's Office, Child Unit, Closed Investigations/Case Disposition Report. The "Closed Investigation Report" from the Middlesex County Child Abuse Prosecution Unit indicates the following reasons for "NO PROSECUTION": Child incompetent to testify, Insufficient Disclosure/Evidence, Child unwilling to testify, Family unsupportive of investigation/prosecution, Victim moved from jurisdiction, No Case Jurisdiction, Perpetrator unknown, Re-

solved without prosecution, Therapeutically inappropriate, Beyond statute of limitations.

50. Plato, *Apology*, trans. F.J. Church (New York: Macmillan Publishing Company, 1956), 22.

51. 1990 HBO Movie Presentation: *Judgement. Judgement* is the story of Father Gilbert Gauthe, the first Roman Catholic priest prosecuted in the United States for the sexual abuse of children. Between 1972 and 1983, Father Gauthe molested 70 (or more) boys; the Louisiana diocese had knowledge of Father Gauthe's activities and ignored them. Finally the parents of several abused boys took legal action. The quote cited, "They're just boys, they'll be fine" was part of a conversation between the fathers of two boys involved in the law suit. One father wanted to convince the other to accept the $200,000 settlement offered by the church; the settlement terms prohibited criminal and/or future civil prosecution. The second father refused; their family lawyer succeeded in winning civil damages of over a million dollars; subsequently Father Gauthe was prosecuted and sentenced to prison.

Information regarding Father Gauthe, pedophile priests, and the response of the Roman Catholic Church can be located in the *National Catholic Reporter*, Vol. 21, No. 32, 07 June 1985 and Vol. 24, No. 11, 08 January 1988.

52. Catherine, survivor. Written account shared with author.

53. Faith, survivor. Excerpted from written account shared with the author.

54. Herman, *Father-Daughter Incest*, 23.

55. Gail Elizabeth Wyatt and Gloria Johnson Powell, editors, Lasting Effects of Child Sexual Abuse (Newbury Park, 1988), "Hidden Victims, Hidden Pain," by Roland C. Summit, 40. Summit cites the work of D. Hechler, *The Battle and the Backlash: The Child Sexual Abuse War* (Lexington: Lexington Books, 1988).

56. *Ibid.*, 40.

57. For information on the effects of child sexual abuse, the following resources may be helpful:

*Thou Shalt Not Be Aware: Society's Betrayal of the Child* by Alice Miller. Miller provides a synopsis of Freud's early clinical findings regarding the symptoms in patients reporting childhood sexual experiences. (pgs. 107-118)

*Secret Survivors: Uncovering Incest and Its Aftereffects in Women* by E. Sue Blume. Blume provides "The Incest Survivors checklist" of characteristics compiled from her work with survivors. (pgs. xviii-xxi)

*A Sourcebook on Child Sexual Abuse* by David Finkelhor. Finkelhor reviewed the "Initial and Long-Term Effects" of child

sexual abuse. (pgs. 180-198)
*Child Sexual Abuse: New Theory and Research* by David Finkelhor. Finkelhor provided an extensive summary of the effects of child sexual abuse found in previous research studies. (pgs. 188-199)

58. Armstrong, *Kiss Daddy Goodnight*, 195.
59. Harpo Productions, Inc., "Clergy Abuse," *The Oprah Winfrey Show* (New York: Transcript #784, 14 September 1989), 13. Mr. Shane Earl was sexually abused by Christian Brothers at Mount Cachel Orphanage in Ireland.
60. Excerpt from the journal writings of a 34-year-old adult female survivor of childhood incest. She was abused by her father for over 13 years.
61. A poem written by female survivor on her 30th birthday, prior to the recovery of her incest memories.
62. Page One Productions, *Massachusetts Law In Plain Talk*, Lowell, MA, 30 minutes, 1989, videocassette.
63. ABC News, "Berendzen Pleads Guilty to Obscene Phone Calls," *Nightline* (New York: Show #2348, 23 May 1990), 8. In the course of his interview on *Nightline*, Dr. Richard Berendzen, former president of American University, revealed details of his childhood sexual molestation by a female perpetrator. After experiencing a "post-traumatic" trigger of the abuse in 1987, Berendzen began making obscene telephone calls to women, advertising to do child care in their homes. During the interview, Berendzen described the content of these telephone calls as "quite inappropriate and grotesque."
64. Charlotte Vale Allen, *Daddy's Girl* (New York: Wyndham Books, 1980), 91.
65. Ann, survivor. Letter shared with author.
66. 63-year-old female survivor: from *The Healing of Incest Trauma: Adult Women Survivors Speak*, by Carla Castor-Lewis, presented at the 94th Annual Convention of the American Psychological Association (Washington DC: August, 1986).
67. Katherine Brady, *Father's Days* (New York: Seaview Books, 1979), 194.
68. Poem by 37-year-old female survivor.
69. Bass and Thornton, *I Never Told Anyone*, 181.
70. Poem shared with author.
71. Lucy, survivor. Question asked of author.

## Chapter Four

1. Stephen Bies, survivor. *The Looking-Up Times*, Vol. 7, No. 1 (Augusta, ME: Spring 1991), 5. Stephen Bies specifically requested that his full name be used to identify his writing. For Stephen,

anonymity suggests that he is ashamed of himself for what someone else did to him; and it has been a matter of central commitment for him to stand up against that shame and challenge public misconceptions about survivors.

2. Stephen Bies, survivor. Written account shared with author.
3. Pat, survivor. Poem shared with author.
4. Rush. *The Best Kept Secret*, 16-17.
5. Susan Brownmiller. *Against Our Will* (New York: Viking Penquin, Inc., 1976), 281.
6. *Ibid.*
7. Genesis 19:32. All Biblical quotations in Chapter Four are from the Revised Standard Version.
8. Brownmiller. *Against Our Will*, 281.
9. Leviticus 18:6.
10. L. William Countryman. *Dirt, Greed and Sex* (Philadelphia: Fortress Press, 1988), 162.
11. de Mause. "The Evolution of Childhood," *The History of Childhood* (New York: Peter Bedrick Books, 1988), 45.
12. Eva C. Keuls. *The Reign of the Phallus* (New York: Harper and Row, 1985), 275.
13. *Ibid.*, 276.
14. de Mause. "The Evolution of Childhood." 43-44. de Mause quotes from Aristotle's Politics p. 81.
15. John Boswell. *Christianity, Social Tolerance, and Homsexuality* (Chicago: The University of Chicago Press, 1980), 81 and 144.
16. Countryman. *Dirt, Greed and Sex,* 147.
17. *Ibid.*, 35.
18. New Catholic Encyclopedia. Vol. 7. (Washington, D.C.: McGraw-Hill, 1967), 420.
19. Mark 9:42 and Matthew 18:6.
20. David Herlihy. *Medieval Households* (Cambridge: Harvard University Press, 1985), 26. Herlihy quotes St. Augustine's *Confessions.*
21. *Ibid.*, 27.
22. *Ibid.*
23. *Ibid.*
24. Roland C. Summit. "The Child Sexual Abuse Accommodation Syndrome." (*Child Abuse & Neglect* Vol. 7, Pezamoa Press, Ltd., 1983), 188-189.
25. Herlihy, *Medieval Households,* 37.
26. *Ibid.* Also, *Butler's Lives of the Saints,* Vol. May, has a story about St. Dymphna's life and death.
27. New Catholic Encyclopedia. Vol. 4 (Washington, D.C.: McGraw-Hill, 1967), 1130.

28. Lisa Cahill. *Between the Sexes* (Philadelphia: Fortress Press, 1985), See discussion of Aquinas' theory of Sex and the Law of Nature, p. 106-108.
29. Judith Dwyer. Interview by Jade Angelica, 06 Dec 1989.
30. Philippe Aries. *Centuries of Childhood* (New York: Random House, 1962), 107.
31. *Ibid.*, 100.
32. *Ibid.*, 102.
33. *Ibid.*
34. de Mause. *The History of Childhood*, 4.
35. *Ibid.*, 5. de Mause quotes from Aries p. 105, but alters the wording a bit. Note (36) is an exact quote from Aries. Although both responses are outrageous, the difference between "smiled" and "roared with laughter" is signifcant.
36. Aries. *Centuries of Childhood*, 105.
37. *Ibid.*
38. *Ibid.*, 103.
39. de Mause. *The History of Childhood* (New York: Peter Bedrick Books, 1988), 49.
40. *Ibid.*
41. *Ibid.*
42. Judith Lewis Herman and Emily Schatzow. "Recovery and Verification of Memories of Childhood Sexual Trauma," in *Psychoanalytic Psychology.* (Lawrence Erlbaum Associates, Inc., 1987), 1.
43. Rush. *The Best Kept Secret.* See Rush's discussion of "A Freudian Cover-Up," p. 82-85.
44. *Ibid.*, 83.
45. *Ibid.*, 82-85. de Mause. *The History of Childhood*, 49.
46. *Ibid.*, de Mause.
47. Virginia Woolf. "Hyde Park Gate." (*Moments of Being*, New York: Harcourt Brace Jovanovich, 1985), 168 and 177.
48. Louise de Salvo. *Virginia Woolf* (Boston: Beacon Press, 1989), 303.
49. *Ibid.*, 2.
50. *Ibid.*, 305.
51. John Crewdson. *By Silence Betrayed* (Boston: Little, Brown and Company, 1988), 25.
52. *Ibid.*
53. Alice Miller. Her book, *The Drama of the Gifted Child*, was the first of its kind to talk so frankly about the effects of childhood abuse on the victims. Her later books, *Thou Shalt Not Be Aware*, and especially *For Your Own Good* provide more details as well as case studies highlighting the effects of childhood abuse.
54. de Mause. *The History of Childhood*, 1.

## Chapter Five

1. Jade C. Angelica, *We Are Not Alone: A Teenage Girl's Personal Account of Incest from Disclosure through Prosecution and Treatment* (Somerville, MA: Justice For Children, Inc., 1992), 1. "Jane" is a fictional character based on interviews with and observations of teenage victims of child sexual abuse within the Massachusetts Justice System.
2. Daniel, survivor. Daniel was a victim of satanic ritual abuse in childhood. His written account was shared with the author.
3. The National Council of the Churches of Christ in the United States of America, A POLICY STATEMENT: *Family Violence and Abuse* (November 14, 1990).
4. The National Committee for the Prevention of Child Abuse, *For the Love of Children: A Resource Packet for Religious Leaders on Child Abuse Prevention* (Chicago), 2.
5. Dee Whyte, Massachusetts Children's Trust Fund, interview by author (Boston: 2 October 1992).
6. Malcolm C. Burson, Celia Allison Hahn, Douglas A. Walrath, Peggy Day, Diane Bowman, *Discerning the Call to Social Ministry* (New York: Alban Institute, 1990) inside front cover.
7. Debra Rossbach, Safe Kids Program, "Congregational Pilot Project Summary," (Cleveland: June 1989), 4-5.
8. *Origins* Vol. 22: No. 7, "Canadian Bishops' Committee. Fifty Recommendations: The Church and Child Sexual Abuse" (Washington, DC: The Catholic News Service, 25 June 1992), 99.
9. Father Joseph Guido, O.P., interview by author (Cambridge: 15 October 1992).
10. *Origins* Vol. 22: No. 7, "Canadian Bishops' Committee. Fifty Recommendations: The Church and Child Sexual Abuse," (Washington, DC: The Catholic News Service, 25 June 1992), 100.
11. *Origins* Vol. 22: No. 16, "Chicago Policy Regarding Clerical Sexual Misconduct With Minors," (Washington, DC: The Catholic News Service, 1 October 1992), 275.
12. *Ibid.*, 276.
13. *Ibid.*, 275.
14. Father Joseph Guido, O.P., interview by author (Cambridge: 15 October 1992).
15. *Origins* Vol. 22: No. 16, "Chicago Policy Regarding Clerical Sexual Misconduct With Minors," (Washington, DC: The Catholic News Service, 1 October 1992), 276.
16. *Ibid.*, 277.
17. *Ibid.*, 282-83.

18. *Origins* Vol. 22: No. 7, "Canadian Bishops' Committee. Fifty Recommendations: The Church and Child Sexual Abuse," (Washington, DC: The Catholic News Service, 25 June 1992), 97.
19. *Ibid.*, 100.
20. *Ibid.*, 104-105.
21. *Ibid.*, 106.
22. *Ibid.*
23. *Ibid.*, 99.
24. Reverend Lucinda Duncan, "The Meeting House News," Vol. XLV: No. 15, (Cambridge: 23 September 1992), 1.
25. Reverend Lucinda Duncan, telephone interview by author (Cambridge: 13 October 1992).
26. Unitarian Universalist Association General Assemblies 1977 and 1985. General Resolutions.
27. Lisa Lightman, telephone interview by author, (Cambridge: 29 October 1990).
28. Reverend Libbie Deverich Stoddard, telephone interview by author (Lafayette, IN: 4 April 1990).
29. CBS Narrator, Ted Holmes, "She Shall Overcome: Religion and the Struggle for Women's Rights," broadcast on 27 September 1992.
30. Peggy Halsey, *Abuse in the Family: Breaking the Church's Silence* (New York: National Division, General Board of Global Ministries, The United Methodist Church, 1990), 1.
31. Gloria Steinem, dustcover review of *Secret Survivors* by E. Sue Blume.
32. *National Catholic Reporter*, Vol. 24: No. 11, 08 January 1988.
33. *Ibid.*
34. Kellie Pini, *Case Analysis* (Somerville, MA: Middlesex County District Attorney's Office, Child Abuse Prosecution Unit, 9 January, 1992).

**Chapter Six**

1. Resolution 7-15A of The Lutheran Church-Missouri Synod. "To Encourage Synodical and Congregational Support for Prevention of Child Abuse." July 24, 1992.
2. *Origins* Vol. 22: No. 7, "Canadian Bishops' Committee. Fifty Recommendations: The Church and Child Sexual Abuse," (Washington, DC: The Catholic News Service, 25 June 1992), 107.
3. Nancy, survivor. Written account shared with author.
4. Lee, survivor. Written account shared with author.
5. Terri, survivor. Written account shared with author.
6. Elaine Westerlund, *Responding to Incest: In Memory of Nancy* (Boston: Women in Crisis Committee, The Episcopal Diocese of

Massachusetts, 1987), Preface by Reverend Anne Carroll Fowler, 2.

7. Linda T. Sanford, interview by author, 29 December 1989, Somerville, MA.

Also, Kellie Pini, *Case Analysis* (Somerville, MA: Middlesex County District Attorney's Office, Child Abuse Prosecution Unit, 5 January 1991).

8. Victoria Bolles and Leora Zeitlin, editors, *Promise the Children* (Boston: Unitarian Universalist Service Committee, 1989).

9. The cost of group therapy will vary by geographic location and will certainly increase every year. Generally, therapists charge each group member (groups usually have 6 - 10 members) $30 - $40 per 2-hour session. The cost estimate for a group sponsored by a religious community is obviously lower with the hope that a therapist would conduct a group for $100-$150 per session. Without incurring the cost of office space, this would be a reasonable fee for a therapist by 1992, East-coast standards. To keep the cost down, the group could be 8 weeks in duration, or 1 hour in length. Usually, survivor groups are co-led, but in many situations, one therapist can be sufficient. Usually an interview with the therapist is required before participants are accepted for the group. Fees for the interview time should also be factored into the budget. A word of caution: this is intense, serious therapy work. Make certain the therapist you choose is qualified to be working with this population. An unqualified therapist can actually do more harm.

## Chapter Seven

1. Eve, survivor. Written account shared with author.
2. Linda, survivor. Written account shared with author.
3. Massachusetts Attorney General Scott Harshbarger, excerpt from speech delivered at a meeting sponsored by the Children's Trust Fund (Boston: 21 October 1992).

## Appendices

1. Jane Walsh, Assistant District Attorney, interview by author, 8 November 1989, tape recording. (Middlesex County District Attorney's Office, Child Abuse Prosecution Unit, Somerville, MA.)

2. National Committee for the Prevention of Child Abuse, "For the Love of Children: A Resource Packet for Religious Leaders on Child Abuse Prevention" (Chicago: NCPCA, 1990), 4.

3. National Committee for the Prevention of Child Abuse, telephone interview by author, 4 February 1991, Chicago.

4. David Finkelhor, "Mistakes Found in National Child Abuse Study Statistics: Westat Releases Revised Estimates for 1986," *The Advisor* Vol. 4: No. 1 (Winter, 1991), 9.

5. *Ibid*.

6. Linda T. Sanford, interview by author, 29 December 1989, Somerville, MA.

7. Kellie Pini, *Case Analysis* (Somerville, MA: Middlesex County District Attorney's Office, Child Abuse Prosecution Unit, 5 January, 1991).

8. Maya Angelou, *I Know Why The Caged Bird Sings* (NY: Random House, 1970). Katherine Brady, *Father's Days* (NY: Seaview Books, 1979). Charlotte Vale Allen, *Daddy's Girl* (NY: Wyndham Books, 1980).

9. Annie Lally Milhaven, editor, *Sermons Seldom Heard: Women Proclaim Their Lives* (NY: Crossroad Publishing Co., 1991), 23-27.

# Selected Bibliography

Angelica, Jade. *We Are Not Alone . . . A Teenage Girl's Personal Account of Incest from Disclosure through Prosecution and Treatment.* Somerville, MA: Justice for Children, Inc., 1992.

Angelou, Maya. *I Know Why The Caged Bird Sings.* New York: Random House, 1970.

Aries, Philippe. *Centuries of Childhood: A Social History of Family Life.* New York: Random House, 1962.

Armstrong, Louise. *Kiss Daddy Goodnight.* New York: Pocketbooks, 1979.

Bass, Ellen and Louise Thornton, editors. *I Never Told Anyone: Writings by Women Survivors of Child Sexual Abuse.* New York: Harper & Row, 1983.

Berrick, Jill and Neil Gilbert. *With The Best Of Intentions: The Child Sexual Abuse Prevention Movement.* New York: The Guilford Press, 1991.

Blume, E. Sue. *Secret Survivors: Uncovering Incest and Its Aftereffects in Women.* New York: John Wiley & Sons, Inc., 1990.

Boswell, John. *Christianity, Social Tolerance, and Homosexuality.* Chicago: The University of Chicago Press, 1980.

Brady, Katherine. *Father's Days: A True Story of Incest.* New York: Seaview Books, 1979.

Brock, Rita Nakashima. *Journeys by Heart: A Cristology of Erotic Power.* New York: Crossroad Publishing Company, 1988.

Brown, Joanne and Carole R. Bohn, editors. *Christianity, Patriarchy, and Abuse: A Feminist Critique.* New York: The Pilgrim Press, 1989.

Brownmiller, Susan. *Against Our Will: Men, Women and Rape.* New York: Viking Penguin, Inc., 1976.

Burson, Malcolm, et. al. *Discerning the Call to Social Ministry.* New York: The Alban Institute, 1990.

Butler, Sandra. *Conspiracy of Silence: The Trauma of Incest.* San Francisco: New Glide Publications, 1987.

Cahill, Lisa. *Between the Sexes: Foundations for a Christian Ethic of Sexuality.* Philadelphia: Fortress Press, 1985.

Conte, Jon R. *A Look at Child Sexual Abuse.* Chicago: National Committe for Prevention of Child Abuse, 1986.

Countryman, L. William. *Dirt, Greed and Sex: Sexual Ethics in the New Testament and Their Implications for Today.* Philadelphia: Fortress Press, 1988.

Crewdson, John. *By Silence Betrayed: Sexual Abuse of Children in America.* Boston: Little, Brown and Company, 1988.

de Mause, Lloyd, editor. *The History of Childhood: The Untold Story of Child Abuse.* New York: Peter Bedrick Books, 1988.

de Salvo, Louise. *Virginia Woolf: The Impact of Childhood Sexual Abuse on Her Life and Work.* Boston: Beacon Press, 1989.

Film Distribution Center. *Breaking Silence.* (Videocassette, 60 minutes). Seattle, WA: Film Distribution Center.

Finkelhor, David. *Child Sexual Abuse: New Theory & Research.* New York: The Free Press, 1984.

_____. *A Sourcebook on Child Sexual Abuse.* Beverly Hills: Sage Publications, 1986.

_____. "Sexual Abuse and Its Relationship to Later Sexual Satisfaction, Marital Status, Religion and Attitudes." *Journal of Interpersonal Violence* Vol. 4 (1989).

Fortune, Marie M. *Sexual Violence: The Unmentionable Sin.* New York: The Pilgrim Press, 1983.

Gelinas, Denise J. "The Persisting Negative Effects of Incest." *Psychiatry* Vol. 46 (1983).

Gravitz, Herbert and Julie D. Bowden. *Guide to Recovery.* Holmes Beach, FL: Learning Publications, Inc., 1985.

Herman, Judith. *Father-Daughter Incest.* Cambridge: Harvard University Press, 1981.

_____. *Colloquium: Sexual Violence.* Wellesley, MA: Wellesley College, The Stone Center. No. 83-05 Work in Progress, 1984.

Herman, Judith and Emily Schatzow. "Recovery and Verification of Memories of Childhood Sexual Trauma." *Psychoanalytic Psychology.* Lawrence Erlbaum Associates, Inc., 1987.

Horton, Anne L. and Judith A. Williamson, editors. *Abuse and Religion: When Praying Isn't Enough.* Lexington: D.C. Heath and Company, 1988.

Keuls, Eva C. *The Reign of the Phallus: Sexual Politics in Ancient Athens.* New York: Harper & Row, 1985.

Lanning, Kenneth V. *Child Molesters: A Behavioral Analysis.* Quantico, VA: Behavioral Science Unit, Federal Bureau of Investigation, 1986.

Lew, Mike. *Victims No Longer.* New York: Nevraumont Publishing, Co., 1988.

Maguire, Edward Ross. *Profile of the Pedophile: A Critical Research Review.* Salisbury, MA: Independent Research Study, 1990.

Maltz, Wendy and Beverly Holman. *Incest and Sexuality: A Guide to Understanding and Healing.* Lexington, MA: D.C. Heath and Company, 1987.

Middlesex County Child Abuse Project. *Massachusetts Law in Plain Talk.* Produced by Suzanne White, Directed by Ruth Page. (Videocassette, 30 minutes.) Page One Productions, Lowell, MA: 1989.

_____. *The Child Abuse Reporting Law: The Middlesex County Experience.* Cambridge: Middlesex County District Attorney's Office, 1986.

Milhaven, Annie Lally. *Sermons Seldom Heard: Women Proclaim Their Lives.* New York: The Crossroad Publishing Company, 1991.

Miller, Alice. *The Drama of the Gifted Child.* New York: Basic Books, Inc., 1981.

_____. *For Your Own Good: Hidden Cruelty in Child Rearing and the Roots of Violence.* New York: Farrar, Straus, Giroux, 1983.

_____. *Thou Shalt Not Be Aware: Society's Betrayal of the Child.* New York: Meridian, 1984.

Peters, David B. *A Betrayal of Innocence: What Everyone Should Know About Child Sexual Abuse.* Waco, TX: Word Books, 1986.

Pini, Kellie. *Case Analysis.* Somerville: Middlesex County District Attorney's Office, Child Unit. 5 January 1991.

Poling, James Newton. *The Abuse of Power: A Theological Problem.* Nashville: Abingdon Press, 1991.

Roth, Nicholas. *Men Who Rape: The Psychology of the Offender.* New York: Plenum Press, 1979.

Rush, Florence. *The Best Kept Secret: Sexual Abuse of Children.* New York: McGraw-Hill Book Company, 1980.

Russell, Diana. *The Secret Trauma: Incest in the Lives of Girls and Women.* New York: Basic Books, 1986.

Sanford, Linda T. "Pervasive Fears in Victims of Sexual Abuse." *Preventing Sexual Abuse,* Vol. 2 (1987).

_____. *But You Hide It So Well: Adult Survivors of Physical and Sexual Abuse.* June, 1988. Tape recording of lecture.

_____. *Family Dynamics of Sexual Abuse.* June, 1988. Tape recording of lecture.

Schatzow, Emily and Judith Herman. "Breaking Secrecy: Adult Survivors Disclose to Their Families." *Psychiatric Clinics of North America,* Vol. 12, No. 2 (June, 1981).

Stoddard, Libbie Deverich. "Not in My Family: Some Issues of Sexual Abuse." Lafayette, IN: 1988. Sermon.

Summit, Roland C. "The Child Abuse Accommodation Syndrome." *Child Abuse and Neglect.* Vol. 6, 1983.

Vale Allen, Charlotte. *Daddy's Girl.* New York: Berkeley Books, 1980.

Westerlund, Elaine. *Responding to Incest: In Memory of Nancy.* Cincinnati, OH: Forward Movement Publications, 1987.

Woolf, Virginia. *Moments of Being.* New York: Harcourt Brace Jovanovich, 1985.

Wyatt, Gail and Gloria Powell, editors. *Lasting Effects of Child Sexual Abuse.* "Hidden Victim, Hidden Pain: Societal Avoidance of Child Sexual Abuse." By Roland C. Summit. Beverly Hills: Sage Publications, 1988.